DETERMINED TO RISE

How 16 Women Transformed Their
Biggest Challenges Into Powerful
Opportunities For Growth

Queens In Business

DETERMINED TO RISE
How 16 Women Transformed Their Biggest Challenges Into Powerful Opportunities For Growth
© 2021 Queens In Business

ISBN: 9798428520750 Paperback

Edited By: Sunna Coleman

Cover Designed By: Tanya Grant - The TNG Designs Group Limited

The strategies in this book are presented primarily for enjoyment and educational purposes. Every effort has been made to trace copyright holders and obtain their permission for the use of copyright material.

The information and resources provided in this book are based upon the authors' personal experiences. Any outcome, income statements or other results, are based on the authors' experiences and there is no guarantee that your experience will be the same. There is an inherent risk in any business enterprise or activity and there is no guarantee that you will have similar results as the author as a result of reading this book.

The author reserves the right to make changes and assumes no responsibility or liability whatsoever on behalf of any purchaser or reader of these materials.

Acknowledgements

By Chloë Bisson
Founder of Queens In Business

As a female entrepreneur, we are faced with many ups and downs. Entrepreneurship is a rollercoaster ride and for me, the one thing that makes it all worthwhile is the ladies on the rollercoaster sat right next to me.

Firstly, I want to say thank you to my co-founders; Carrie, Shim, Sunna and Tanya. You all continue to inspire me every single day and I feel grateful to have you all by my side, as business partners, as friends and as family.

I want to give a special thank you to Alex and Gaby, our amazing team behind the scenes, who have worked tirelessly to get this book into your hands.

I want to give a special thank you to Tanya for her beautiful artwork for this book and helping us to turn our vision for the image of the QIB Club into a reality.

I want to give a special thank you to Sunna, our Chief Editor, who has supported our authors, helped us craft every word and transformed our stories into the inspiring chapters you're about to read.

Finally, I want to give a special thank you to you, the reader, for taking the time to read this book and continuing to give us a reason to share our message with the world!

Dedication

This book is dedicated to all the women who have decided that their struggles, fears and hardship will not limit or break them, but shape them to become stronger. With this attitude, we all grow.

With love,
Queens In Business Club

Table of Contents

Introduction

No matter who you are, where you come from and what type of life you lead, we all experience moments of fear, sadness and hopelessness at times. That's the nature of life - it comes with plenty of challenges, difficult decisions and roadblocks.

When we are faced with obstacles, especially life-changing ones, it can be a struggle to keep positive and to keep going. Sometimes, all we want to do is give up or hide away from the world. And that's OK, for a little while...

But we can't stay that way. We can't let our toughest moments break us if we want to rise to a new level.

We all have a choice.

We can either let life's challenges hinder us from ever being brave again, from ever being happy again, from ever having hope again... or, we can use our experiences to learn something more about ourselves and our strength.

We all have the ability to transform our difficult moments into powerful opportunities for growth. And there are important lessons to be taken from everything that we face - the good and the bad.

Using our resilience as fuel, we can move forward with more purpose and drive than we ever imagined. Because we won't let life get in the way of our mission and the people we strive to help.

In this book, you will discover inspiring stories from sixteen female entrepreneurs who have come together to share their most challenging experiences in life and business. Taking you on their personal journeys, they uncover exactly how they overcame difficulties again and again, to stay connected with their drive to succeed.

In reading these stories, we hope that you will find the belief and power within yourself to heal from any setbacks and move forward, determined to rise.

Defeat Is Optional

Sunna Coleman
Blogging for Business Coach
Bloggers Inspired

"The more I exercise it, the more natural it becomes to not let my fears run me" --- Arianna Huffington

I was waiting in the shadows. My heart was beating hard. Everything around me was muffled as if I were shrinking away into my own world, somewhere I'd be safe.

"Breathe into your stomach" - voice coach Carrie Griffiths' words came back to me. Deep breath in, deep breath out. Deep breath in, deep breath out... As the breathing exercise began to ease my nerves, the sound of Carrie's voice on stage flooded back into my ears.

"Please welcome Sunna Coleman!" Music blared, the audience burst into applause and Carrie stood expectantly, waiting for me to walk into the light and take the mic.

My legs started moving, I reminded myself to smile, to enjoy this moment, and suddenly there I was. The music stopped. The audience fell into silence. And under the glaring spotlights, I could barely make out any faces in the crowd as I stood up there alone. But I could feel the energy. Every single person in that room of 100 was waiting for me to speak.

What the *hell* was I doing??

From The Page To The Stage

I'm a writer. And I'm a writer for a reason. In writing, I feel like I can express myself fully and eloquently. As a child, I discovered that I could process thoughts and feelings I didn't understand through writing - whether diary entries, poems or songs. Writing is my thing.

I am the writing expert for the Queens In Business Club, Editor in Chief of our magazine and of lifestyle and career blog, Inspired in the City. I'm also a writing and blogging coach for students, aspiring content creators and female entrepreneurs. Once I found my strength, I was quite happy remaining firmly within its borders.

Speaking is a whole different ball game. Give me a blank page and I can fill it within seconds. Give me an audience and I crumble. My mind goes blank, my mouth dries up and I stumble over my words, unable to string them together.

I do not feel comfortable speaking. But I have always admired people who can hold a room's attention with interesting discussion and argument. Deep down, I wondered why I couldn't achieve this myself. What was so different about writing the words vs speaking the words? They both involve the very same thing: words.

Being passionate about helping people with their writing skills, I wished I was more confident to put myself in the limelight in order to reach more people - whether by speaking on social media lives, in a lecture room full of students or on a business stage. But I resigned myself to the idea that speaking just wasn't for me.

This became a bit of a problem when, in 2020, I was approached to deliver an online talk for the University of Roehampton on the subject of blogging. My heart was saying, "Absolutely yes!" - it was my dream to be able to inspire the younger generation. But my head was saying, "You can't do this, you're going to make a fool of yourself."

Luckily for me, my dad has instilled us with the belief that any dream of ours is possible and that following them is always the right thing to do. So without hesitation, I took the offer and panicked later.

How on earth was I going to talk for an hour? Why would they want to hear from me? I'm rubbish at presentations, I'm going to regret saying yes. All the usual limiting beliefs ran through my head like crazy. So I turned to what I know best: writing.

I wrote pages and pages and pages of notes. My answer to smashing this talk was to have every possible point written down in front of me so that there was no way my mind could go blank and leave me in silent embarrassment. I spent hours deliberating over every word. At last, I was set.

Or so I thought.

A few weeks before I was due to give my talk, I joined a Zoom meeting with five other ladies who had come together to launch a little something called the Queens In Business Club. On this call, we were to record our first video together, welcoming our future members into the club.

Of course, I had made notes. So I simply read them out when it was my turn to talk. But, if you know the other Co-Founders, you won't be surprised to hear that they instantly called me out for doing this and made me do it all over again - this time trying not to read my notes. Thanks guys.

I just wanted it to be over, but I tried again. Still not good enough (this tough love is something we now all appreciate about each other - it's what keeps us continually becoming better versions of ourselves).

This time, they urged me to try speaking without my notes by my side, and they promised that they would use the previous takes if it didn't work out. That sounded like a reasonable deal to me, so I went for it.

Wow. Without my notes there, I felt an instant change in the way that I was speaking. It was far more natural and I sounded more comfortable (even though inside, I was screaming).

My fellow Co-Founder, Carrie Griffiths, is an incredible voice coach, and she explained to me that relying on notes actually restricts you from speaking more naturally because you're more focused on following exactly what you've written. By taking the notes away and trusting yourself, you allow yourself to speak more freely, in a conversational way - which is more engaging for the audience. I couldn't believe that this simple shift had worked on me so quickly.

I had a lot to learn from these women. I told them about my upcoming talk and they had one more invaluable piece of advice for me: shift the attention away from yourself and onto your audience. That means, forget about your own ego and remember that you are there to help others. What do they need from you? What can you teach them?

As I left that meeting, I was eager to apply what I had learned. I revisited my extensive notes for the Roehampton talk and edited them down. It felt completely wrong to remove my safety net and risk having nothing to say if I freeze up, but I put faith in what I had learned and experienced on that Zoom call.

And it worked! When the day of my talk finally came, I was so close to adding more notes onto my slides but I reminded myself of what I needed to do. I focused on the audience and not myself, I trusted my knowledge on the topic, and I used that to fuel my confidence when delivering my talk.

After it finished, I was elated. I was so grateful that I had stepped out of my comfort zone, taken a leap of faith in my ability and put into practice the advice that I had been given. It all paid off.

Most of all, I was proud to have been able to inspire those young students and empower them to build their own opportunities in life. I would never have been able to reach them as effectively as I did if I had stayed hidden behind my writing.

We Are Reflections Of Our Community
I never truly understood the power of surrounding yourself with the right people until I co-founded the Queens In Business Club. I have certainly never lacked ambition or drive and I thought that was enough to get me where I want to be in life.

What I didn't realise I was missing, is the amazing feeling of joint accountability, motivation and support that you get when you're part of a community of people whose values and mission align with your own so closely.

It's a whole different experience. Being your own cheerleader is important, but realistically is hard to keep up. It's all good when we are in a positive and happy state, but we're only human - sometimes we're going to have moments of doubt, worry and sadness. And when we're down, it takes a huge amount of energy and strength to keep ourselves motivated and moving.

Being part of the Queens In Business community has completely transformed being in business for me. I just have to look around me to see incredible women on their own journey to freedom and success - each figuring it out in their own way. If they can do it, I can do it. It re-energises me to keep pushing on.

My biggest challenge this year? Stepping out from behind the keyboard and in front of an audience. It was important for me to get over my fear. I knew that by doing so, I would open up more opportunities for myself. Not only that, but if I wanted my business to be seen by more people online (something that was vital when everything went digital during the pandemic), I needed to get a grip of social media lives and videos.

On video, you can portray your personality far more easily than through writing. This helps you connect with your audience more, attracting your ideal clients and filtering out those whose values won't gel with your own quite so well. In an age of content overload, it's super important to find ways for you and your business to stand out among the noise. You won't be able to do this if you're going to look and sound just like everyone else. Generic won't cut it. Hiding behind the keyboard won't cut it.

I knew all this, yet my fear of speaking was holding me back. I needed to get used to putting my personality out there so that I could connect with more people. And seeing other women in the Queens In Business Club going live on social media, being unapologetically themselves, I was feeling inspired to do the same.

Watching their examples, I realised that I wasn't sat there judging them for how they speak or how they look. I was just grateful that they were sharing their knowledge with the world. Like them, I needed to remember to shift focus away from my ego and any self-conscious thoughts, and towards my audience and what they needed from me.

So I finally tried broadcasting a Facebook Live. And I honestly don't know why I used up so much time and energy worrying about this stuff. It was so easy!

Now that I was armed with the right mindset, I flew through it with relative ease. The nerves were still bubbling under the surface but I was learning how to control them. It may sound small to some, but I couldn't believe that I had just overcome a fear that had been holding me back for so long.

On a high, I steadily practised using mindset shifts to improve the way that I presented online. I was pleased with my progress and I couldn't wait for my confidence to grow further.

Then, I was told I'd be speaking live on stage. Sorry, what?

To mark the end of our first year running Queens In Business Club, we were organising a two-day event in London, inviting female entrepreneurs to hear from top speakers from around the world. As part of the event, the Co-Founders would all be given a slot on stage, including me. I've never spoken to a live audience on stage at a big event before, why were they trusting me to do this? Only a few months ago I had never even done a Facebook Live!

I was quite happy learning to overcome my fear of speaking at a gradual and steady rate. Sharing a stage with some of the industry's top speakers was a monumental jump. I was nowhere near ready!

But my Co-Founders clearly had faith in me. I'd trusted them on this before, and I had survived to tell the tale. Perhaps, it would do me good to trust them once again - even if I thought they were all absolutely crazy.

My slot on stage was to run a panel discussion, interviewing some of our club members on the topic of female entrepreneurship. As a journalist, I had interviewed people for work all the time, so that settled my nerves a little. But only a very, very little.

How on earth was I going to pull this off?

And that's when I caught myself. I needed to get out of 'limiting belief mode' and use the mastery of mindset. I *can* do this. I am going to use this opportunity to help others in the best way that I can. I will do this for myself. I will do this for others. I have experience interviewing people, and I trust myself. I'm excited to do this!

Your Perspective Can Free Or Imprison You

You know when you tell yourself you're going to have a bad day, and then you do? That's because our brains are built to prove themselves right. When you allow yourself to think negatively, and convince yourself that you're going to have a bad day, your mind works to prove you right, pointing out all the things that could be interpreted as 'having a bad day'. It's called confirmation bias.

Knowing this, it's extremely important to practise keeping a positive mindset whenever possible to help things work in your favour.

When I was told that I would be speaking on stage in front of a room of 100 people, I panicked. That's OK. It's a normal reaction for someone who is uncomfortable and unaccustomed to doing so. But it's how I then processed this panic that was more important and vital to my success.

I reminded myself that my worries stem from my own ego - what if I mess up, stumble on my words, look stupid? But, although the spotlight would be on me, being on stage isn't actually about me at all. It's about who I'm there to serve: the audience. Therefore, my focus should be on them - how can I help, how can I deliver my message, what do they need from me?

It's a super powerful mindset move.

I also reminded myself of how mindset has helped me in other areas of my life. One such example was during the pandemic, when we were cut off from seeing the majority of our friends and family. I was recently married and had just moved in with my husband to the county that he lives in. I was away from almost everyone that I knew and when he had plans to see friends, I was stuck. Travelling far from home was not advised at the time.

I have never been someone who enjoys their own company. My family home had always been busy, with someone there at all times. I wasn't used to being completely by myself - in fact, I hated being alone. On rare occasions where no one would be home but myself, I'd quickly make plans to meet someone.

But I couldn't do this in the pandemic. I resented being left alone in my new flat, in an area that I didn't know. Then I came across the book Alonement: How To Be Alone and Absolutely Own It by Francesca Specter. I realised that the reason I hated being alone was because of my mindset around what it means to be alone. I connected being alone with negative thoughts. If I could learn to shift this, and use being alone as a positive time to indulge in me, myself and I, then I could learn to like it - love it even.

And that's exactly what happened. After over 20 years of convincing myself that I just wasn't the type of person who likes to spend time alone, I had flipped my belief on its head.

Taking control of your mindset can really set you free.

Everything Is Impossible Until It's Done
Speaking on stage at our event in December 2021 was not perfect. I had never done anything like this before, there were no rehearsals, no space for messing up, no chance to hit delete if it all went wrong. I couldn't see the audience with the spotlights glaring at me, I stumbled over a word or two, my leg was shaking - I even had a wardrobe malfunction! The only pair of tights I had packed had a hole in them. Thank god for the black eyeliner trick…

Despite all this, I have never been more proud of myself. I actually did it. I faced my fear head on, and guess what? It is true what they say - the fears we build up in our minds are far worse than the reality.

By letting go of the pressure and the idea of being perfect, I was able to encourage myself to embrace this opportunity. Who actually cares if I mess up slightly every now and again? It makes me more relatable and human. Have you ever been "perfect" at something the first time you tried it? It takes practice. But you can't practise, without doing something for the very first time when you start.

So I wasn't perfect, but I really wasn't terrible either. I was kind of good! Impressive, in fact, if you take into consideration that I was way out of my depth. And now that I've done it once, I know I can do it next time and be even better.

By working on my mindset, I gave myself a solid foundation of confidence-inducing tools to be able to take that leap and speak on stage. And the best thing about it all, is that I can apply this magic to any challenge or fear that I face.

So whatever is holding you back in life or business right now, consider how you can change your perspective. What happens to your emotions and sense of self when you start telling yourself you *can* do something? What limiting beliefs can you flip upside down?

Sometimes the biggest hurdles we face are within ourselves. But the great thing about this is that *we* have the power to change it.

To help you along the way, find your community. Surround yourself with people that inspire you and use that energy to motivate yourself, tapping into positive mindset practice to give yourself the best shot at everything you want to achieve.

When you're ready, I'll see you on the other side of fear.

About Me

I am a content marketing specialist and Founder of Bloggers Inspired, helping small business owners escape social media overwhelm and take back control so that they can stand out from their competitors.

I have always believed that I can be anything that I want to be. That's how my dad brought us up. My mum's parenting style was centered around safety - she taught us to make good decisions, look for security and find happiness grounded in reality. My dad was the dreamer - no goal is too big, take the risks you need to, because you are capable of anything.

With a healthy balance of both world views, I was well equipped to follow any career path I set my heart on. That was never a problem for me. What I wasn't as prepared for, were the hurdles that begin to appear the closer you get to your biggest dreams.

In business, it's not enough to be an expert in your industry, you need to get yourself and your message out there if you really want to reach and help thousands of people.

As Editor in Chief of lifestyle and career blog, Inspired in the City, I have worked with global brands including the likes of Revlon, Ted Baker, Boohoo, Hotel Chocolat and Desenio. Having taken an untraditional route to break into the journalism industry, I faced a lot of challenges and prejudice. When no one would give me a shot, I used blogging to create my own portfolio to prove myself. And now, with almost a decade of industry experience, I am passionate about raising awareness of the power of blogging in business and career. I have spoken at university events alongside representatives from the BBC, ITV, C4, CNN, Disney and Warner Brothers.

As part of this, I launched Bloggers Inspired, a programme to help female entrepreneurs attract more clients, convert more sales and create brand loyalty through the marketing power of blogging for business. But in order to keep this growing, I need to continue to pick up new skills that I didn't anticipate. Things like accounting and sales - I've never been a numbers person. Things like speaking on camera for social media - no surprise here that I'm far more comfortable writing than I am speaking.

Growth for me is all about overcoming my fears and never telling myself that I *can't* do something. It's about being open to change and training your mind to think in ways that it's not used to. There are always solutions for you if you are willing to look.

I'd like to dedicate this chapter to my husband, Terry, who always supports me in everything that I decide to take on and gives me the time and space to work on my dream. I really appreciate you.

From Pain To Purpose

Shim Ravalia
Award-Winning Entrepreneur, International Speaker,
Gut Stress Expert and Founder
The Gut Intuition

"As you grow older, you will discover that you have two hands, one for helping yourself, the other for helping others"
-- Maya Angelou

Have you ever had a time in your life when just a bit of information could completely change your outlook and make your future look uncertain?

I remember it all too vividly. It was during a cold day in January 2018, and I had just come home from helping out at a workshop. I was no longer working in my sports therapy business. No longer driving in every day, keeping up with client demands and looking after a growing team.

I just didn't love it anymore. It wasn't fulfilling. So a part of me was relieved when I closed the business - the stress of running it lifted away. But that was just the surface. Deep down I was unhappy, not fulfilled and kind of just floating about doing bits and pieces for someone else. At the time, it suited me just fine - to turn up, do the work and get paid for it. The minimal responsibility felt bloody great and I found myself drawn back to the simplicity of it.

Then that cold day in January, I walked through the living room, took off my coat and dropped my bag to the side. My whole family was sitting there in silence and I immediately thought I'd done something wrong.

The silence felt like five minutes. And then my sister spoke and told me to sit down because dad had some news to tell me.

I sat down slowly next to my dad and looked over at him. He was sitting at the edge of the sofa, looking down at the floor and seemed lost in thought. It was my brother who spoke next, "Dad's neuro consultant called and basically said he has got six months to live."

I remember this moment so clearly. It was the moment where my true growth and transformation started. I looked over at my dad and said in a soft tone, "Dad, do you believe you have six months to live?" He replied with a simple, "No."

We both made eye contact and understood the truth. As much as I loved him for telling the whole family what we wanted to hear, I could see it in his eyes, his tone and his body language that he had already checked out, that he had accepted his illness and that was that.

Five months later on June 13th, dad left this world and moved onto his next mission. It was one of the saddest days I have ever felt in my life so far. Prior to his passing, we had the best time together. We had heart to hearts over bottles of red and got a little tipsy at times. I became his personal rehabilitation specialist at home, making him do strengthening exercises every day. The look on his face when I got him to do squats and shoulder raises was hilarious, like a child throwing their toys out of the pram.

We would often laugh about it together too. And you know what the best thing was? We created memories together that I'll cherish forever and it instantly puts a smile on my face every time I think about him and his grumpy face! Haha!

But what would you do if you were told you only had six months to live?

When my dad was faced with this, the thought sent shivers down my spine and made me question what the hell I was doing with my life. You see, I've had "realisations" before and they were always somewhat softer but this question actually haunted me - in a positive way. It made me question everything. I mean EVERYTHING, from health to wealth to my environment, relationships, connections and what truly made me happy.

This is the strange and beautiful thing about grief. Whether it's losing a loved one, loss of a relationship or a breakdown within yourself, heartbreak creates this darkness that, at times, can make you feel like it's difficult to breathe. It's a real deep sense of melancholy and nostalgia which always brings a tear to my eye. However, I've come to know grief in a different way - although there is darkness, there is another door opening with an opportunity waiting to be accepted. My dad's passing was the opportunity, the gift to truly go after what made me happy, to find out what my purpose was and to understand it.

Journey Into The Unknown

Nobody told me the journey was going to be a tough one. I mean, I knew what steps I needed to take but actually the scariest part was embracing the unknown.

For the first time in my life, I didn't put work or business first. I made a brave choice to put health right at the top of everything else. With no real income, it was a risk I was prepared to take and had to get comfortable with. It wasn't the easy choice but it was the right choice for me.

My health was actually at its worst by December 2018 and I was really burned out with pain from head to toe which caused an imbalance in me. I knew it was only going to get worse and worse if I carried on. It was actually quite weird to just focus on my health and nothing else but I went with it and trusted my intuition.

Having to go back to the drawing board to get rid of what *used* to work for my body and figure out what works for my body *now* was a painful process. It's undoing all the years I spent in the health and fitness industry, always staying on top of the latest course, exercise convention, latest gadgets and gym workouts. But I didn't give my body the same respect and treatment in keeping it in a healthy state.

I had to go through massive transformation and I realise now that my mess became my message for you today. This painful journey is what led me to create my second business, The Gut Intuition. Listening to my intuition and just embracing the unknown were one of the two key ingredients for the success of my business today because it allowed growth to happen in the way it needed to happen.

The beautiful thing was, the more I went with the flow and worked with my health and my body, the more things in my new business were just slotting into place. Things like, knowing what my logo was going to be, what the colours I have chosen meant, my core values, my purpose and my 'why'. These were not easy things to answer but I remember having so much fun putting my plan together that time just didn't exist at all.

That's when I knew I was in harmony with myself and my surroundings - things just made sense and 'clicked'. I felt true peace knowing that everything was going to be OK, whatever hurdles and challenges came my way.

Accepting Growth Comes With Pain
At this point, I would like to invite you to stop reading for a moment, grab pen and paper, and write down all the painful moments, situations and realisations you've had over the years. On the other side, write down what you've gained from each obstacle. What transformation did it create for you?

The reason why I want you to do this is to simply remind you of the fact that growth cannot exist without pain (read that again).

Think about it for a moment… Babies go through pain as new teeth form. Before a butterfly is created, the caterpillar has to go into a cocoon phase. When finances are limited, it creates pain to do something about it. When training for a marathon or a mountain, the practice is grueling. The list can go on and on.

This is how growth really stands out for me:

G - Grief. Going through grief of losing a loved one, loss of a relationship, burdens, losing something valuable which creates pain.

R - Realisation. The key pivotal moments hitting home like a jolt running through your body, out of your control and pushing you to think much deeper.

O - Opportunity. Taking the opportunity to see the gift in the situation and getting comfortable with risk.

W - Way. Looking at a way forward to the future in doing what's right and not what's easy.

T - Transformation. Making changes to become a better version of yourself where the process challenges you in ways you were not expecting, but you embrace it anyway.

H - Harmony. Having a real sense of peace after going through the transformation. Knowing that everything will be OK no matter what happens.

When you zoom out and have a look at the above, you can start to understand that one doesn't come along without the other.

So in order to truly have the result you want, you have to go through some level of pain to create that growth necessary for that transformation. I mean, Arnold Schwarzenegger didn't win five Mr Universe and six Mr Olympia titles just by doing a few squats here and there. He did the uncomfortable, embraced the unknown and followed it all the way through without giving up. The results speak for themselves.

Now, I know the typical response to pain would be: "Ouch, I'm never doing that again. I'm just going to play it safe."

In my humble opinion, playing it safe all of the time actually leads to more pain. Looking at pain in a different way helps you shift, move forward, and makes you think in a different way. The fundamental thing I've learnt about pain is that, without the darkness, you wouldn't be able to see the stars.

Here's how I believe pain can give you a different perspective and help you deal with it in a healthier way:

P - Purpose. The more you avoid finding out your purpose on this planet, the more painful life becomes because you just end up following the herd. So, always reflect back on whatever you do and ask yourself, what's my purpose and am I in alignment with it? Make it a daily practice.

A - Acceptance. When you can accept a situation or a set of circumstances for what it is, it allows you to find some peace within yourself rather than constantly trying to fix it or find a million ways to avoid or change it. Acceptance can also create awareness and accordingly, you are able to create a brand new experience for yourself.

I - Intuition. It's something you are born with and the less you use it, the more you suppress it. The best advice I can give you is to never ignore your intuition, even when it's telling you something you don't want to hear. The best thing to reflect on is where you are using your logic and where you are using your intuition. Is there an equal balance between the two?

N - Natural. The more you don't play to your natural strengths, the more pain you end up creating, shunting your growth. In managing my businesses, I tend to be a multitasker, thinking it's a great thing to do and even feeling proud of it. However, you don't actually grow like this. In fact, you end up diluting your strengths and burning out. So, don't focus on your weaknesses, play with your strengths and delegate the rest.

Trust me, you will be much happier for it.

About Me

I am the Founder of The Gut Intuition and Co-Founder / Head of Operations & Growth for the Queens In Business Club. I help business owners and entrepreneurs go from stressed to success in health and in business.

I've had the pleasure of being featured in many well-known publications like Business Woman Today, CBS News, Fox, NBC and ABC to really spread my message and my vision about health for the future of entrepreneurs all over the world.

Born and bred in East London, I have always been curious about the human body and the mind. I came away from university with two degrees in Sports Rehabilitation and from here I worked in gyms and leisure centres until I found my entrepreneurial path...

Being part of this book with so many incredibly strong, forever growing female entrepreneurs is an absolute true honour. Growth is a fundamental part of entrepreneurship, but growing together is extremely empowering.

I dedicate this book to my dad who gave me the best gift a daughter could ever ask for, finding her true purpose.

The Greater The Storm, The Brighter The Rainbow

Chloë Bisson
Two-Time #1 Best-Selling Author & Multi-Award
Winning Female Entrepreneur
Queens In Business

"I trust that everything happens for a reason, even if we are not wise enough to see it" -- Oprah Winfrey

It was 2015. I was lying in bed looking out the window at the crisp and bright morning. My alarm went off, I hit the snooze button again and all I could feel was my stomach churning.

I ran to the bathroom and hovered over the toilet but nothing happened. I'd felt queasy all week but no matter how many times I ran to the bathroom, I couldn't be sick.

On the way to work I called up the clinic and booked an appointment with my doctor. Dr. Redshaw had been my family doctor for over ten years. She was incredibly understanding and had the patience of a saint so, as she asked me what I was visiting for, I opened up for the very first time.

"I'm constantly feeling sick. Every morning I wake up and my stomach is in knots and I have to force myself to get out of bed. As soon as the evening comes, the sickness has gone but I'm absolutely exhausted. I'm constantly tired no matter how much I sleep."

In the past I had suffered with a lung condition and troublesome cough due to too much acid in my stomach and so I thought she would just prescribe the same tablets as she did before. But I couldn't have been more wrong.

"It sounds to me like you may be suffering with depression, Chloë."

I'm sorry, what? Depression? I'm the most positive person I know! There was no way she could be right. What could I possibly be depressed about?

I've got my dream job. I've been travelling around Europe. I've just moved into a beautiful new flat. There was no way she could be right. All of these thoughts were flying through my mind.

"I'm going to sign you off for the rest of the week and I'll give you a call on Friday to see how you're doing," she said. I honestly thought she'd gone mad. "Over the next few days, spend some time reading these leaflets and we will talk on Friday."

I don't think anything she said after that actually registered in my brain. I was in shock.

"It's going to get worse before it gets better Chloë, but you'll get there."

Flashforward 12 months, and boy was she right. I'd been signed off work with severe clinical depression for six months, lost my job, lost my home and felt like I'd completely lost myself.

But I honestly believe that when you have nothing more to lose, you realise everything that you have to gain, and my determination was born.

Determination is the fuel that gets you through the hardest of times. The energy to push through what life throws at you, no matter what - that's real determination.

I was fortunate enough to have a very supportive network of loved ones, family members and friends that helped me to find my feet again, step-by-step. The more determined I was to get through it, the more determined I became for more. The need for survival turned into the need for growth.

I went from just wanting to be able to get out of bed in the morning to wanting to do more with my life. To use my new-found awareness and motivation to help other people every single day.

The Highs And Lows
When people ask me, what's been the biggest driver for my growth, I answer… "Starting a business."

I truly believe that there's no better way to grow within yourself than starting a business. Most female entrepreneurs have the passion to run their own business but many underestimate what it actually takes.

Whether it's learning where to find clients, how to sell, what systems you need, what social media platforms to be on, how to build a team... there's so much learning to do!

And starting a business has a way of challenging you in every aspect of life, it puts you in situations that challenge every core human need and make you question things you'd never questioned before. And there's a reason for that.

Because the bigger the challenges, the bigger the achievements. The higher the highs as they say. It takes true determination to walk away from the stability of "the norm" and not be 100% certain of where your next paycheck will come from.

To put yourself out there to the world, be vulnerable and open yourself up to the opinions and judgements of others. The strength and determination to face all of that and start a business is an investment in your future.

The buzz and excitement for what you're creating, the freedom to choose what you do for work, when you work and who you want to work with. Not to mention the highs of people paying you what you're worth and having unlimited earning potential.

Accepting the highs and lows of entrepreneurship is part of growth. Challenging my norm and pushing myself out of my comfort zone, that was the beginning of my growth.

Surviving Your Growth

Growth in business can come in many forms: increase in income, more clients, new products, more team members.

As a 'numbers' person, I could give you every £ or % you need to know to grow your business, but if I'm honest, none of it matters without personal growth.

People often ask me how I've been able to achieve so much at such a young age and the answer is simple. Personal growth. When you work on yourself, truly learn about yourself and dig deep, your growth opportunities are truly endless. Because you remove or reduce the one barrier that often stops female entrepreneurs from rising: themselves.

Many female entrepreneurs will invest in their own growth by getting a mentor or attending a course to learn a new skill. Many female entrepreneurs also invest in their business growth by putting money into paid advertising or recruiting more staff. But if they don't commit to their personal growth, there will be a disconnect, and for many of them, their growth will even come crashing down.

Imagine the foundations of a house and three groups of bricks - personal, professional and financial.

Personal   Professional   Financial

The goal is to have equal bricks in each area to ensure your house is stable, just like your business.

As you learn new skills and develop your business, you will be laying more bricks in the professional area.

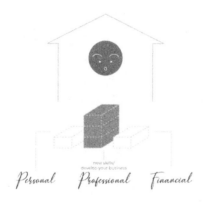

new skills/
develop your business

Personal   Professional   Financial

As you get new clients and make more sales, you will be laying more bricks in the financial area.

Personal   Professional   Financial

But if you're trying to build your house on those foundations, without adding bricks to the personal area, the house will break.

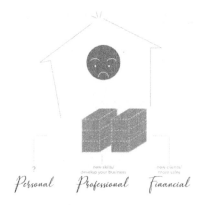

Personal   Professional   Financial

To be able to build a stable house, you must be conscious not to leave any of the three areas behind. Laying an equal amount of bricks in all three will get you the sturdy dream house that you have been yearning for.

Personal   *Professional*   *Financial*

There are many stories of extremely successful entrepreneurs growing their business, having it all and then out of nowhere, losing it all.

It's because their personal growth didn't match their professional and financial growth.

For example, you may start to grow your business, win more clients and suddenly earn more than you've earned before. But, if your mindset isn't aligned with that, or there's a part of you that doesn't feel you truly deserve it, there's a high chance that you'll subconsciously find a way to reduce your financial growth.

Maybe buying something that you don't need, spending the money as soon as it comes in, or even accidentally breaking something that causes you to use that money on fixing the "unexpected" problem.

If your professional and financial growth levels don't align with your personal growth levels, your mind will be forever trying to keep your professional and financial growth down, to keep it all in balance.

No matter how hard you try, you can't break that cycle. The key is to stop working on your professional or financial development and start spending time on your personal development.

- Who are you under the surface?
- What's important to you?
- What are your core values?
- What drives you?
- Why do you want to grow?
- What will it do for you?
- What needs to happen for you to allow yourself to grow?

These are just a few questions to get you started.

Finding My Tribe

For me, realising my vision or mission wasn't like an epiphany moment that just hit me like many people experience. It was something that came to me in 2020 whilst running my training and coaching business.

I was sat in a coffee shop in London, sipping on my mocha as I was catching up with an old friend. She was one of the rare friends that ran her own business and also had her own history of mental illness. So, to say we had a lot in common was an understatement.

She was always really excited about my plans and ideas and I told her about my new idea to launch a membership club for female entrepreneurs. As I sat talking to her about my ideas for this club, all of the awesome training, the regular mentoring sessions, the live events, it suddenly dawned on me. It was way too much for me to do on my own.

Not just because of my already back-to-back schedule but because the idea of this club was bigger than just me. And that's exactly what excited me about it.

As the conversation moved on, I tried to concentrate on what she was saying, but all that was going around in my head was that I couldn't achieve this vision on my own. The birth and growth of this incredible community would only be possible if I allowed myself to let others in to help me. That wasn't a decision that I mulled over for weeks. In fact, it was a matter of minutes.

As I left the cafe, sun shining on me, I walked home through the park and all I could think about was who could help me make this dream a reality. Then, out of nowhere, without a doubt in my mind, I knew as clear as day who it would be.

Now I don't know exactly what it was - the universe, a guiding spirit or a god - but whatever it was, it just gave me their names. It was like an indisputable feeling, like a divine download from someone, somewhere, telling me exactly who to ask.

And similar to the way I do most things, I didn't think, I didn't wait, I just took action and I messaged them all:

"Hey lovely! I hope you're well. I've got a really exciting opportunity that I was hoping to talk to you about! It's super top secret at the moment but I'm launching a new exclusive club for female entrepreneurs. It's going to be an online and offline club that focuses on providing support, training and community for female entrepreneurs."

"But I'm very much aware that the best things come from collaborations and I want this community to be bigger than just me so I'm looking for experts to join me in this venture as exclusive partners. Each of the experts will be specialists in different areas of business and I was wondering whether you'd be interested in being one of those partners? If you're interested, let me know and I can run you through my thoughts, how it will work and the benefits x"

There. It was done.

Within three hours, I'd come up with the idea and invited a handful of incredible women, many who didn't even know each other, to come along on the ride with me.

Without even knowing at the time, that was one of my biggest moments of growth as a female entrepreneur. The moment I truly accepted that I couldn't do it on my own.

Looking back, we all laugh about it now. They all knew me quite well and knew that I had a strict boundary in my business that I don't work weekends. It's something I put in place a long time ago to look after my health. But this particular Saturday, in my excitement and new-found alignment, I sent them all the message.

Most of them panicked, thinking, "What's Chloë doing messaging me on a Saturday? Something must be wrong!"

And within only a few hours, every single one had replied, "Heaven yes!" …well not exactly those words but all different variations of, "Of course, I'm in!"

I'd given them hardly any information, literally just a dream and an invitation. They all did one of the most powerful things a female entrepreneur can do… Say YES and work it out later.

They had no idea what they were getting themselves into, neither did I at the time! But they followed their hearts, trusted their gut and opened themselves to the opportunity.

Since then the Queens In Business Club has opened its doors to over 100 female entrepreneurs, launched 18 different courses, run two virtual summits, published its own magazine, launched its own merchandise, run its very first live event, Reign Like A Queen and published two number one best-selling books... in only a year.

And all of that's only been possible because I realised I couldn't do it all on my own.

I believe the more determined you are to grow, to rise, to achieve, the more frequent the challenges you will face. So the need for determination never really stops. Not because you're not good enough, not because you don't have what it takes, but because you're striving for more.

There is no end point to growth. It's not like in a computer game when you reach the top level and all the enemies vanish. There's no finish line.

Female entrepreneurship isn't a career path, it's a life choice. It's a part of your DNA. It's that undeniable feeling that you deserve something more. That you have more to give to the world. That you were born for something more. And listening to that feeling, leaning into it and saying HEAVEN YES.

That's true growth. That's the key to rise.

About Me

If there is only one thing you need to know about me, it is this - I believe that all women have what it takes to be successful female entrepreneurs and that women have the right to create their own businesses, their own income streams and their own happiness.

Also known as The Automation Queen, I manage multiple six and seven figure businesses and am a two-time number one best-selling author, an international speaker and multi-award winner.

As a chartered accountant at the age of 21 and director by the age of 24, my success came to a sharp halt when I was diagnosed with severe clinical depression at the age of 25. After months of growth and recovery, I knew I was meant for more than just the normal path and began my journey of entrepreneurship.

Since then, I've been featured on the cover of Global Woman Magazine, spoken on stage alongside Kim Kiyosaki and been featured on BBC, Fox, ABC, NBC, CW, London Business Magazine, Business Woman Today, Foundr and some incredible media outlets.

Today, I run two global training organisations and am a Co-Founder of the Queens In Business Club, a training organisation that teaches female entrepreneurs how to build successful businesses. To date, we have helped thousands of women build their own businesses and make their dreams a reality!

Knowing When To Say 'NO'

Carrie Griffiths
Voice and Transformational Coach
Carrie Griffiths Voice Training

"I knew then that victories were always just the other side of tragedy" -- Chrissie Hynde

Trigger Warning: domestic violence

According to Harvard Business Review, people with a growth mindset believe that their talents aren't simply gifts that they either have or don't have, but are skills that can be developed.

People with a growth mindset "tend to achieve more than those... who believe their talents are innate gifts."

I have always believed that I have a growth mindset. As a lifelong learner, I always valued education, believing academia was my ticket out of the council estate, my ride to success. And to some extent, it was. I proudly took course after course, and eventually did a music degree before completing teacher training at Master's Level.

As a singer, I achieved more than I ever thought possible, selling out numerous venues, gathering fans around the world, performing to audiences of tens of thousands, and even selling a number one album.

As a teacher/lecturer, I worked with a lot of private training companies, helping them to improve the quality of their teaching and educational resources. I was even headhunted and asked to set up a math and English education department for a high-end hairdressing company.

I had a lot of fun and ticked a lot of boxes. I built up a large friendship group and became known as someone who likes to have fun (I do). I worked hard, played hard, and loved hard. I grew to like my own company and loved living by myself.

Then one day, I stumbled upon Bob Proctor and learned about paradigms and how they dictate your thoughts, behaviours and results. That was the day that I stood up and faced the music, and admitted that despite it all, I was inherently sad and pretty lonely.

Being a high achiever at school led me to believe that I would be a high achiever in life. Until that day, I had bought into the systemic lies, truly believing that academic success equalled success elsewhere. I realised that I had, naïvely, believed the hype.

Simultaneously, this realisation answered a lot of questions. I had already spent many years searching for answers as to why - despite being a high achiever on paper - I couldn't settle with a decent partner or provide a long-term home for myself.

To give you a better picture, I'd like to take you back to the winter of 2011…

It's around 10pm on a cold December night in London. I'm hiding in a bush, waiting for the police to come and get me. There's blood streaming from my head and I'm feeling woozy.

I think he's gone but I'm too scared to come out in case he sees me.

I'm shivering with a combination of cold, fear and anger when the police finally arrive. There are four or five of them but I can't quite focus. The female officer asks me questions while another takes my coat and puts it in a bag for evidence. They call an ambulance to take me to the hospital…

When I wake up in the morning, I have no recollection of what has happened. I know I had told the police that he hit me round the head with a wine bottle, but I don't know who was drinking the wine. I vaguely remember the police asking me if someone had cut my hair – I answered, "No, he hit me with a wine bottle."

There are no shards of glass in my head but I have two open wounds, one of which has been glued together.

I have just £1.35 to my name - enough to catch one bus. But I live in Fulham and I'm on the other side of London. I can't get home with £1.35.

I check my phone and my friend has texted, telling me to go to her house. How does she know that I need help? My head is sore. I'm still woozy from the alcohol and the blows to the head, and I can't walk at my usual brisk pace.

My phone battery is almost dead but I manage to ask the nurses which hospital I'm in and realise I can get a bus most of the way to my friend's house and walk the rest of the way. I text her back, telling her I'm on my way but in bad shape and I don't know how long it will take me to get there.

The recollection above is not a scene from a soap opera. This is one episode from an extremely abusive relationship. I was in that relationship for less than two years but when I look back, it bore all of the signs of extreme toxicity from very early on.

Although that was the last physically violent act I experienced during that relationship, it wasn't the last in a string of abusive incidents (yes, I STILL went back to him after that).

I have since recalled that he hadn't hit me with a wine bottle. He held me by my hair and smashed it repeatedly against the radiator. His mum came into the room and marched me out of the flat. He had run after me and I managed to hide in the small bushes nearby.

For years, the right-hand side of my head was almost completely numb - the same side of my head that I shave when I have an undercut. My stammer worsened, as did my memory, and as I write this, I still experience random headaches, particularly in cold weather.

I have two sensitive scars, one at the back of my head, and one on the top.

Fast forward to 2022, and when I'm feeling stressed, I feel a dull ache around these scars, I get a sharp headache across the rest of my head and my right eye feels like it might pop out of its socket. But on the positive side, the pain has lessened over the years, and I have recovered most of the feeling on the right side.

The Unknown Truth

The thing about domestic violence that most people don't realise, is that by the time the violence occurs, you are so caught in the grip of the relationship that it's not always as easy to leave as you would think.

It took me a long time to come to terms with what happened during that time. Having been branded "intelligent", I often wondered over the years why I put up with so much. People have told me how stupid I am for staying for so long. Others have blamed me for getting back with him the dozens of times we "split up" (you never truly split up until you have no contact). Each time, I come to the same conclusion: I was brainwashed.

He was so loving, so "perfect" at the beginning of the relationship that, even when I was in fear for my life, metaphorically and literally, I clung desperately to the hope that he would snap out of whatever evil had taken over him and that my soulmate would reappear. It's this hope that keeps victims and survivors in abusive relationships.

Looking back, I can see how I slowly became the perfect candidate to be caught in the lair of an abuser. But more importantly, I am able to share how I have finally overcome the emotional scars of that relationship. I can share how I came to truly accept myself and my shortcomings so that I can do what I was put on this Earth to do.

First Steps
The harsh truth is that pretty much my whole identity relied on validation from others - it was a hard lesson to learn. I had been blind to it my entire life, believing I was beating my own path and flying my own flag. But nothing could have been further from the truth.

Although I grew to be happy in my own company very quickly after leaving boarding school, whenever there were other people around, the performer in me craved attention from everyone. Any removal of that attention felt like a stab in the heart, another rejection and more proof that I wasn't good enough.

And when I started taking my first business seriously, this insecurity took hold with two large hands! It would take years to understand and acknowledge just how lost I was and find a light in the darkness.
I had spent years navigating the music business and all of the bullsh*t that goes with being a woman in the industry. I was

approachable and friendly while quietly seething, fighting to be seen and heard without being seen as just a pair of tits on stage. When I survived it all and decided to give up performing, along with all of the crap I had gone through as a child, I thought I could deal with anything.

But I had no clue just how difficult it would be to build a business with all of this baggage weighing me down.

Now that I was around very successful entrepreneurs and business owners, my own achievements paled into insignificance. I was so desperate to be accepted as a "professional" that I became a fraud. Not because I wasn't an expert in voice and vocal training, but because I lied to myself about my own worth.

I had spent so long unfairly comparing myself to millionaires and multi-millionaires and telling myself I didn't know enough that I eventually believed my own lies and bought into them. I believed those lies as much as I had believed that I would become a successful singer all those years before, when I was living in a dead-end town in the South of England.

But my biggest mistake was adopting goals that other people told me I should be achieving, rather than setting my own. Despite being fully booked just three months after starting my voice coaching business, I was so ashamed of the mistakes I'd made in my personal life that I no longer trusted myself to make the right decisions. I looked to my coaches and mentors for guidance and (unfairly) took what they said as the only truth.

Maybe you've been in a similar position? Perhaps you've been so desperate to get as far away from your mistakes as possible, or to do things the "right" way, that you've lost yourself and become someone you don't recognise. I know now that that was a process I had to go through.

I spent a long time desperately scrambling to work out what I wanted and find my place in the world of entrepreneurship. I learned a lot during those two years. But my biggest growth came when I finally forgave myself.

A Lesson In Self-Acceptance
They say that you can forgive without accepting, but for me, the reverse has been true; I wasn't able to forgive myself - nor my abusers - without accepting that nothing I could have done would have changed the course of those relationships. They were all sent to teach me something about myself, including accepting my own self-worth.

I was diagnosed with anxiety, depression, and passive suicidal ideation in October 2021. It's fair to say I'd been experiencing all three for a number of years but I was in total denial. Even when I heard the diagnosis I told myself I'd snap out of it in a few months.

As I write this in January 2022, I'm doing all the right things: eating properly, exercising, meditation, practising gratitude, daily affirmations, therapy – you name it. I've been doing all of these things since 2016 but it's only now that I've found a way to work through my demons in a more practical way and understand how my "mistakes" have helped me, that I have started to come through the other side.

When you forgive your own mistakes and truly love yourself, everything else starts to fall into place. I speak my truth more than I ever did and I'm OK with people not thanking me for it.

I am finally forgiving myself for having been in so many toxic relationships. I am accepting that I experience depression and anxiety, and forgiving myself for it. And I accept and forgive that I always want the limelight. Ok, to be fair I don't *always* want the limelight, I just want it a lot of the time! Said with my tongue firmly in my cheek, now that I know the difference between healthy and unhealthy attention, and I am able to keep myself safe.

And after years of telling people I didn't care what other people thought, I actually don't care anymore.

True growth is a slow process of inner work. Of accepting your failures. Of accepting your own limits. And accepting that there will be plenty more to come.

For me, growth now also means giving more. More time to listen. More choice. More of myself. More love. More forgiveness. More trust in myself. More "yes" and a lot more "f*ck no!"

I believe that we all have the ability to give and to forgive more than we think we can.

Something I say to my music and singing students is, "Let yourself make mistakes." The mistakes we make in business are different and may be bigger than those you can make on stage - well actually Dave Grohl fell off a 12 feet high stage and broke his leg in front of 52,000 people – that's pretty big! So if you're going to make a mistake, you may as well make it a big one and learn some big lessons.

As an Artist Development Coach, I am finally helping the very people I set out to help when I realised I had a business. This has been three years in the making.

I've been a chameleon in life, adapting to my surroundings, even when the environment was hostile and unfriendly. But now I am more like a butterfly.

My advice to everyone who is riding the rollercoaster of business is: accept yourself, forgive yourself, love yourself. You're worth it.

About Me

I am the Founder of Carrie Griffiths Voice Training, and a London-based leading voice coach, specialising in commercial singing, and conversational and public speaking.

Having been a successful singer for more than twenty years, I have performed in over thirty countries to audiences of thousands, and sold three top ten albums, including a number one.

I have used these experiences to create a fun and simple voice training system that helps voice workers to reconnect with their voice so that they can regain control and sing or speak with more strength, stamina and power, and create engaging professional presentations and performances.

I love to help creatives from musicians to designers, to writers to monetise their talents without confusion, overwhelm, or working ridiculous hours.

Grow Through What You Go Through

Tanya Grant
Brand Specialist, Founder & CCI
The TNG Designs Group Limited

"Never underestimate the power you have to take your life in a new direction" -- Germany Kent

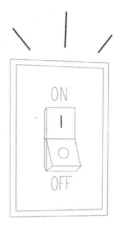

What needs to change in order for you to make a move?

Read that a few times. Take it in.

Now ask yourself the question. I mean really ask yourself and actually take the time to figure out what the answer is for you. Especially if there is one thing you've been keeping on the back burner for way too long.

That same question was asked of me one week before I wrote this chapter and when I think about it, my answer is what's been helping me to keep moving all these years.

There have been a few phrases and questions that have been fired at me and have stuck with me along my discovery journey. They've been my motivation to take action and grow.

I know growth's typical meaning is to increase in size but when we use it to describe life, I believe it to be about increasing in knowledge and the way we take action with it. That includes everything that we've learnt from past experiences, occurrences, people's behaviours as well as our own and more. It's at each of those pivotal moments where our 'time to move' button gets triggered and switched on, so that we do exactly what we should do… move

In this chapter, I get to take you on a journey that will further explain why I am that healthy mix of stubbornness and sheer determination I spoke about in Queens In Business Club's first book, Time To Reign.

One thing you'll get to know about me is that I never claim to be a unicorn or unique in the stories I tell about myself. What I will say however, is that I'm sure many of you will resonate with me about a few things that I'm about to tell you. What I will be sharing, is how, with that healthy dose of stubbornness and sheer determination, I *chose* to move forwards and I *chose* me whilst doing it too.

And if you're thinking about that last part… no… choosing you isn't being selfish.

The Rescuer
This is where the growth part of my discovery journey started.

Long before I even knew who I was as an aspiring brand specialist, author, collaborator and public speaker, I'd always put others before myself, and to a certain extent, there's nothing wrong with doing that, but for me, it got unhealthy.

I loved travelling (and still do). Between 2010-2012, you'd often see me dressed up every year, arms flailing and spinning around like a mad hatter in sequins and beautifully coloured tropical feathers, dancing the days away at a carnival somewhere in the world, playing mas (dressing up in costume). I was living my best life and wanted to be in that 'blissful euphoric carnival state'… ALL THE TIME.

I wanted the same for others too.

I was a huge nurturer and always wanted people to just be at peace and happy… ALL THE TIME. I hated arguments and didn't like seeing anyone close to me involved in them… it caused an imbalance in me.

Now, you'd think me feeling that way would stem from having some kind of a turbulent upbringing, but it really wasn't. I actually come from a super close family network that has me in stitches laughing most of the time. So God only knows why I felt I had to take on that responsibility, especially when it wasn't even for me to take on. The feeling like I had to be other people's rescuer I mean.

And this is where it got really unhealthy. I began absorbing other people's feelings and worries too. The minute someone would mention that they were depressed, feeling low or in one hell of a lull or dark space, there I was... Tan to the rescue!

Of course, there is nothing wrong with being there for someone but it's learning how to be there for them where I initially went wrong. And I know exactly where it stemmed from.

You see, during that same 'euphoric' period, I'd found out that a friend of mine committed suicide and I knew of someone else who did the same shortly after that too. That feeling of disbelief, shock, sadness and questioning why they didn't say anything about how they were feeling, especially when I knew they were part of super supportive families and friendship groups - it heightened my rescue mission.

So from there on out, the minute anyone would tell me they were feeling depressed or anything like it, I always wanted to jump straight in there and problem-solve their worries away. And the real unhealthy, all-absorbing part of it was that it made me feel the need to take on their problems too. Now you and I both know that's not how this all works!

It took a long time for me to realise what I was doing and the straw that broke the camel's back was when I sat in my friend Tim's living room feeling as low as he was! He even noticed it and tried pulling me out of it. The rescuer became the rescued!

To be fair, for a time, he was so distracted with the need to help me out, giving me all the positivity he felt I needed to hear, that he forgot about what it was he was going through.

But here's the thing… he eventually slipped back down again. Now I'm no expert in mental health but what I will say is that I have a strong respect for it because of what I experienced. It's my belief that if you let the bad habits of negatively speaking to yourself, feeling like the whole world is against you, or feeling like NOTHING is working get to you, instead of focusing on tools that can help you, then you will find yourself slipping backwards again.

The unhealthy cycle stopped after my experience with Tim. I made the decision to stop because I finally realised that I actually wasn't helping. I made the decision to stop that cycle and choose me.

I had to grow, making that change, and realised that it's the individual's own responsibility to want to make that move for themselves, not mine.

Now don't worry, this hasn't turned me into a heartless person who ignores everyone in a low space. That's not the case at all. The difference in how I now handle things is to simply listen more and to give those who need it the space to be heard.

But here's something that I will never change about me - and you could say that this is another characteristic of that healthy mix of stubbornness and sheer determination. It's the way I help others to feel empowered and motivated to move.

The Learner

It's funny how when you finally stop and reflect, you start to see clearly again and can notice all the things you've been neglecting in your own life.

When I stopped focusing on how everyone else was feeling, it magnified everything else I wasn't looking after. Namely, myself. I could start seeing all the areas in my life where I wasn't showing up, especially when it came to the likes of myself and my business.

You see, as much as I was out there living my best life as a freelancing graphic designer, to a certain degree, when I finally started focusing on me more, that's when I could start seeing all the life size cracks with what I was doing or should I say, wasn't doing. I let the ball drop a lot of the time. Especially where the likes of networking came into play.

For me back then, no networking meant no next job lined up for when a contract had finished. And no next job lined up sometimes meant being out of work for a good month or so.

Sometimes even longer. To be fair, that part actually tired me out. The constant thought of never feeling quite 'settled' I mean.

And when I think back, it's probably why I felt I had to go into full-time employment because I felt that that was how I needed to step it up to finally feel 'settled'.

If you read my chapter in Time To Reign, you'll know how it all panned out with that full-time position. So clearly, it turned out not to be the answer or outcome that I was looking for. But I did learn that I needed something different. I wanted to work for myself.

Albert Einstein said it best… "Insanity is doing the same thing over and over again expecting different results."

So when my hand was forced to leave that full-time position, I knew I had to change old habits and switch it up. I wasn't going to be dropping the ball anymore or waiting on those possible opportunities that often got talked about. I finally decided that it was time to step it up and choose me. I had to, as it was my own responsibility to make it happen for myself.

So, here's what I did…

1. I learnt to drop my old boundaries and build better ones
2. I started showing up more, adding value in the mentorship groups I was in

3. I stopped being the best kept secret
4. I started appreciating the process
5. I became patient with the process

And that about summaries it!

Obviously each of those points are backed by a few years' worth of a discovery journey and then some, but essentially, to get to being the brand specialist as you know me to be today, that's what I did. And those last two points in particular were, at times, my biggest challenges. They were the points that I found the most frustrating.

Why?

Simply because I didn't understand them. And when I mean I didn't understand them, I mean I didn't get the fact that in order to have longevity in all that you do, there's no quick fix or process to get to that point, particularly when we talk about business. What's more, it was actually being OK with it that took a lot of patience.

Just like unlearning 'The Rescuer' complex to be able to grow, I had to learn this process to stir an upward growth in me.

The Giver
When I officially launched my TNG Brand Hub community in the summer of 2020, I went on value overload giving out more than I actually had to. When it came to the likes of my other branded outlets such as my website, social media

platforms, flyers and more, I'd be giving out so much of it, it was like there was no tomorrow!

And here's the thing. The fact that I was giving out value wasn't even the problem, it was the *type* of value that ended up causing me issues.

You see, there are three different types of values that brands or business owners can give away. The first two can be given away for free to your entire audience. But the third, should be reserved for fully fledged clients.

They are…

- The WHAT value
- The WHY value
- The HOW value

The third value is gold dust and it's not to be thrown out there willingly. To be fair it's so easy to let it slip out every now and then! But if you're one of those people giving away too much of the 'how', then do me a huge favour…

STOP SHARING HOW YOU DO IT! Curb that until those you're addressing start paying you!

It took me a while to even figure out how to do that for myself because delivering the 'how' upfront in that 'value trio' became all too much of a natural habit for me. I had to learn the hard way and I know why I used to fall into that trap…

I used to feel like it was my duty or responsibility to give all that information away because it's what I wish I had while starting out in business. Have you ever felt that need…to always 'give, give, give' just because you didn't always get?

But the only person who is really losing out here is you. If you're giving away all the 'how' all the time, then each person whose attention you manage to get will just go away because they've already received all the information that they needed to get. They don't need you anymore if you've already told them how to do what you teach in your business.

When I found myself in that position, here's what I did instead… I chose me. I decided to stop feeling like I 'owed' it to the masses and stopped doing it.

And you know what? As I'm sitting here writing this all out for you, I'm beginning to realise that that same over-giving attitude was how I was showing up in my personal life, with my friends, family and relationships too.

In choosing me, I needed to remember to leave a little something in my reservation tank for myself.

The…
The Rescuer. The Learner. The Giver.

Recognising these points weren't the only times in my life where I had to grow through what I went through but they were the times that I knew something had to change for me to make a move for myself.

And that's the key part right there... for myself.

As a result of each of these scenarios, I knew deep down that I had to be the one to take ownership of my actions. Even when I didn't want to do it, I knew it was my responsibility.

Now don't get me wrong, to get to those stages of realisation, it did require time, help and support. Each of those stages had pivotal trigger moments that switched something on in me and got me to move.

So... with all that being said, especially when you think about that one thing you've been avoiding addressing for waaay too long, break it down and answer that question for yourself again...

What has to change in order for you to make a move?

About Me

The best kept SECRET! That's the one phrase you *don't* want to be known as.

When we're trying to get our businesses and identities known in this vast digital world, being a secret is the last thing you want to be. Ideally, you want to be known as the 'best person for...', or having the 'best solution for...' Right?

When you get to meet me, you'll find out that I will always lead with my values and it's a trait I believe we all should have. As a brand specialist, it's something I always encourage my clients to do too, especially when it comes to tackling their brands.

I've helped thousands of people understand that their values are what will help to drive their brand and message to the masses. This is how you STAND OUT, stop being a secret and start making those authentic connections with the audiences that you actually want to work with.

It's what I did and how I became known as the Branding Specialist who is a naturally solution-based collaborator, best-selling co-author, inspirational entrepreneur, public speaker, award winning content creator, Co-Founder of the Queens In Business Club and the Founder & CCI of a multi-disciplined company, The TNG Designs Group Limited.

I'm dedicating this chapter to all of my nieces and nephews, both blood and non-blood. Know that you are more than the abilities you have.

Anxious To Empowered

Jennifer Roblin
Anxiety Coach, Trainer
and Award-Winning Public Speaker
Founder of Better Your Life

"One can choose to go back toward safety or forward toward growth. Growth must be chosen, again and again, fear must be overcome again and again" -- Abraham Maslow

I want to take you back to 1981. I was 11 years old, at school, sitting in my usual spot at the back of the classroom in the corner.

My English teacher was about to choose the next person to go to the front of the class and read a passage from a book. I was trying to make myself as small as possible so he wouldn't pick me.

Then I hear my name. I could feel my heart racing. My face was flushing. My palms were sweating. I sat rooted in my seat, unable to move. He called my name yet again and told me to come to the front of the classroom, NOW!

I felt that familiar drop in my tummy, that feeling of nausea. I tried to make my way to the front, but my legs were like jelly and I was aware that I was shaking. I stood there awkwardly, trying to find the passage in the book that I was meant to read.

I could sense the classroom was getting bored waiting for me to begin. I knew my face was bright red, as usual. Could they see me sweating? And then I started to read.

My voice was shaking, I stumbled over my words and could hear the other children laugh at me. I tried again but I couldn't make out the words on the page. It was like they were all moving about and all I could focus on was the sniggering from my classmates.

My teacher told me to start again. And again. And again. And again. I couldn't do it. I asked to be excused to go to the toilet and ran out of the classroom before he had time to respond.

That was when I had my first panic attack. I felt weak. My legs couldn't support me. I lay down on the cold toilet floor, certain that I was dying. I couldn't catch my breath. It was like there was no air in the room. I could hear my heart pounding. I felt so scared and so alone, as I lay there shaking uncontrollably with tears running down my face.

I was not sure what was happening to me, but I knew it was bad. It seemed to last forever.

I heard the bell go for break time and the toilet door opened as a bunch of giggling girls came in. I stayed hidden in the cubicle. They were asking who was in there but I stayed quiet. I didn't want anyone to see me. I was a total mess. I didn't want to be seen.

Eventually, someone looked under the cubicle. My cover was blown so I opened the door. One of the sixth form students stayed with me for a while and held me as I sobbed.

Why am I always so stupid? Why can't I do anything right? I am so rubbish. I hate myself.

Family Business

I was particularly quiet that night when I got home from school. My parents could tell something was wrong but I didn't want to scare them and tell them that I thought I nearly died that day. I didn't want to tell them how stupid I was.

I went to bed early and it happened again. As I lay in bed reliving my awful day, the air was sucked out of the room again. I couldn't breathe. I started to shake. My heart was going to burst. Oh no, not again…

My dad came home from work and up to my bedroom to give me a kiss goodnight. He could see that the bed sheets were wet with sweat, my eyes were red and my face was blotchy. I burst into tears and told him what had happened.

He gave me a big hug and told me that we just weren't good at school, we weren't academic. He explained that he hadn't liked school much either, and he was scared of speaking in front of a group too.

Anyway, it was OK because we knew that when I left school, I was going to be a secretary and work for my dad. I would eventually meet a boyfriend, get married and become a housewife, just like my mum. Life was all mapped out. I was lucky because I had a job waiting for me.

It felt good to know it wasn't just me that struggled. My dad, who I really look up to, was the same as me. And he had gone on to set up his own successful business, that my younger brother would one day take over and run. Dad told me I just needed to get through my school years then everything would be OK.

I had always been a shy, nervous child. I was anxious, worrying about one thing or another. I felt everyone else was better than me and I could never measure up to my peers or other people's expectations.

I was short for my age and tubby. I had been given the nickname of Mrs Michelin - as in the logo for the tyre company. I had no confidence in myself. I had a few friends, but I was very shy and didn't really join in much. I kept myself to myself. Sometimes, I tried to be like everyone else but never felt I knew how to. I ricocheted between trying too hard to be liked and not trying at all.

I had a very protected childhood. I had been told that it is very dangerous out in the real world, and my dad would tell me about children that had been murdered or kidnapped because he wanted me to understand the importance of staying safe. I knew I was loved but I would have nightmares about being kidnapped and tortured. Understandably, this didn't help my anxiety!

Stepping Into The Unknown

Fast forward to the end of school and my friend was going to London to speak to an agency about a job. She asked if I would go with her and keep her company on the train. I wasn't allowed to travel to London, I was barely allowed outside of the cul de sac we lived in, so I didn't tell my parents about our plan.

I remember standing on the platform, feeling the rush of air as the train pulled into the station. I felt so grown up and so nervous at the same time. I looked out the window and watched the fields become housing estates and tower blocks. Everything whizzed by so fast, and I was in awe of this other life people lived.

When we arrived at the agency, we were both given a clip board and asked to fill in our personal details. I remember having to sign the form - I didn't have a signature, that was something only grown-ups had. My parents had signed everything on my behalf, so I made one up. I remember the guilt of feeling as if I was forging something.

We were then whisked into an office, asked a few more questions and told to go to Barclays bank that same afternoon. My interview lasted no more than 30 minutes and I was to start my job there one week later. It felt good that I had actually managed to achieve something on my own, I felt a mixture of excitement and nerves.

Then it hit me. Yikes. How was I going to tell my dad? I think he was as surprised as I was that I had landed a job in a bank. After all, the only exam I had actually passed was a typing exam. I think he also thought there had been some kind of mix up and they would need to tell me it had all been a big mistake. He would have prepared me for the disappointment!

Dad came with me on my induction day at work. This seemed perfectly OK with me at the time (I cringe now). I didn't have any confidence in myself and believed I was incapable of doing too much without my dad's help. Looking back, it must have been amusing for my new colleagues!

But I loved working in London. I met my first boyfriend at the bank. He was full of confidence, and it was hard to understand what he saw in me. But slowly, he started to increase my confidence and belief in myself. I also had an amazing boss a few years later. Dave Lowe pushed me outside of my comfort zone whilst always having my back.

I was 24 and was now managing a team, working with hedge funds. Dave wanted me to go to New York to see my clients. He had to be kidding right? Me? Getting on a plane on my own, staying in a hotel on my own. I can't do that. The clients will see right through me and know I have no idea what I am doing, I would end up letting Dave down and I would surely lose my job.

But Dave insisted I went. He told me I can't manage the team and send someone else. I had no choice. As the day got nearer, I was more and more petrified. But Dave gave me a pep talk and I didn't want to let him down.

New City, New Me?
When I got to New York, I was met by a new girl that had recently started working for my client. We hadn't spoken before, but we got on like a house on fire. She took me under her wing, and we did everything together for the next ten days.

I loved New York. By the end of the trip, I called Dave and told him I wasn't coming home! He knew I was serious and arranged a job for me in the city. I moved there three months later.

Life seemed crazy to me. How was it even possible that I was living and working in New York? After all, if you can make it there, you can make it anywhere!

I felt free to be myself in New York. I had to make my own choices and I was responsible for building my own life. Although my confidence was steadily growing, the imposter syndrome remained.

A few years later, Dave asked me to transfer to the bank's Head Office in Stockholm. I was to set a team up and then hand it over to the Swedes to run, so in effect, I would be making myself redundant after a couple of years. I was the

Global Head of my division, and I loved living in Sweden. It was so different from New York. I had some great friends and we spent weekends and summer evenings on my boat in the Archipelago.

By the time I left Sweden, it was no longer quite as daunting moving abroad. So I continued to live and work in several other cities in Europe. I loved building up teams and empowering my staff, and I loved building their confidence in themselves. I learnt a lot about different people and cultures, and what drives and motivates people. I realise with hindsight that I never really lost that imposter syndrome, and I would build my teams up so that I could hide behind them.

It still seems incredulous that I was able to have the life I've had, but it just goes to show that with a bit of encouragement, we are all able to change the things we believe about ourselves.

Somewhere along the way, my panic attacks and anxiety subsided, and I had stopped believing I was stupid. I now had enough evidence to prove differently to myself. I had started to believe that I was capable of doing things on my own.

Getting Out Of My Own Way

After nearly 30 years in banking, I decided it was time to quit. The hours were long and I worked far too many weekends. I wanted to spend more time with my daughter. She was 11 now, and I knew how tough I found it being 11 years old. I thought she needed me more than ever and I wanted to be there for her more.

I took a year off work while I tried to decide what to do next. I am very grateful I had that time to really start to understand who I was and what I wanted. I was able to really reflect on my past and realise that I was 100% responsible for how I felt about myself, and for my own happiness.

My favourite part of my career was coaching my staff, so I went and saw a life coach as I wondered if it was a career I would enjoy. I wanted her to teach me everything she knew about her job.

I wanted to take the leap and set up my own business, but I was too scared. It became clear to me that the only thing holding me back was me.

I had plenty of my own experience of anxiety, and I also had the experience of working with hundreds and hundreds of people within my teams. I had been coaching my teams without really being aware that I was coaching them, and I was able to reflect and realise that the main thing holding us all back was anxiety. It is the fear of being judged by others, the fear of failure and the fear that we are not good enough. I was already an expert in that area!

But I was still getting in my own way of setting up my dream business. I had to just go for it. I had to face my fear and embrace it. I had started my psychology degree in 2005 when my daughter was ten weeks old, and I now knew I loved learning, so I threw myself into more training. I researched everything I could about anxiety. I trained in NLP and neuroscience. I got certified as a Mental Health First Aider, and I went on every course and read every book I felt was relevant.

I set up my company, Better Your Life, in 2016 and soon got my first client. A friend wanted me to work with his dad, who hadn't left the house in three years because he was so scared of having another panic attack. Yikes! Had I taken on more than I was capable of? Those doubts started to resurface, but I knew I could help him.

Our first session was initially held through the open window of his house. Before long, we were going out walking and talking. Walks and talks are such a great way to coach people as there is no direct eye contact and anxious clients find it easier to open up. I knew that talking therapy, nature and some gentle exercise is a winning combination for my clients!

I got more local clients through word of mouth, and I was slowly growing my business. When the pandemic hit, a lot of my coaching calls had to be online, and this helped me realise that my client base was no longer limited to being local. I was loving my job and the feeling of knowing I have helped to improve someone's life is amazing.

Still Playing Small

Whilst I knew I could help my clients with their anxiety, I didn't know anything about running a business. So I got myself a mentor, Jessen James, who helped me to understand that I was still playing small. I had no one to hide behind now, but I was still holding myself back and not growing the business. Jessen helped me understand that it was selfish of me not to share what I knew with more people.

Seeing clients on a one-to-one basis was great, but what about the clients who needed me that couldn't afford one-to-one coaching, or those who preferred a home study programme? So, I created my training course, From Anxious to Empowered.

The course follows my 7 Step Proven Empowered Programme as I was confident that these steps could help anyone overcome their anxiety.

I also realised that while I was encouraging my clients to overcome their fears, I was not facing up to my own fear of public speaking. I had avoided giving any talks or presentations throughout my entire career. I had empowered my teams to take on these challenges instead, so I didn't have to.

It was time to be brave again. Jessen had a public speaking course and I signed up. It was tough at first as I remembered back to my school days, standing at the front of the classroom. I attended the course with some amazing people, and I was still feeling inferior, however I embraced the feeling this time. I was going to use that feeling to push myself and face my fear.

I am now an award-winning public speaker and run my Anxious to Empowered Mastermind events at my Better Your Life Academy.

My Biggest Challenge Was Me

The biggest challenge I had in building my business was me. I was holding myself back because life can sometimes be scary. But it is meant to be that way. We all have a choice. We can stay within our comfort zone, or we can recognise our fears, push on through and grow.

I struggled initially with promoting myself through social media. I felt exposed and worried that people would judge me. Why would anyone listen to what I have to say? But then what right have I got to stay quiet? There are so many people struggling with anxiety and what if my social media post can help just one person? Yes, some people will judge, but that is their problem and not mine.

I was often guilty of finding something so overwhelming, and because I didn't know where to start, I stopped. The key is to break the challenge into bite size pieces, and just start. Once you have managed the first task, you start to build momentum. Your confidence will naturally grow when you look back and see what you have achieved.

I was also guilty of telling myself that I was technically challenged. I now know I can learn anything if I put the time and energy into it, but the thing is, sometimes that is not a good use of my time. If someone can do the one thing I am finding challenging, quicker and better than me, it is OK to outsource it. I have a choice.

No One Needs To Struggle With Anxiety
I wish I was able to tell my younger self that my anxiety would not dominate my life. In fact, it would become a way of recognising how I was feeling, what I was avoiding and why. Knowing that has helped me to grow into the person that I am today.

I now believe that no one needs to struggle with anxiety. Anxiety is evolutionary, it is designed to keep us safe. If we go back a few million years, we really did need to know if there was a tiger lurking in the bushes. We didn't have time to think if we should run, so our bodies have an instinctive fight or flight response. This still serves us very well if we step off the pavement and a car is hurtling towards us. We instinctively jump back on the pavement. Anxiety has the one and only intention, of keeping us safe.

Luckily, we don't have the same life and death situations anymore. But that fight or flight response still kicks in when we have perceived threats. Threats that are in the future that haven't even happened yet. It kicks in when we feel we are being judged by others, because that feeling threatens one of our basic needs, to feel loved and secure. Our fight or flight response makes us question if we did the right thing or makes us avoid a situation all together.

Society now tells us that anxiety is bad. We are put on medication that dulls every feeling we have. We can no longer recognise the happy moments in life. We may not have as much fear, because the meds have blocked that out, but we no longer have as much joy either. We don't have the opportunity to be grateful for the things we love. We feel broken. I'm telling you, we are not broken. We are perfectly great just as we are.

What we do need to do though is unravel our thoughts when we feel fear and anxiety. We need to unravel our beliefs about ourselves that have caused us to be fearful in the first place. I was petrified of speaking in front of a group of people because I told myself I was terrible at it. Because I messed up in school when I was 11 years old. I avoided doing it again for the next 40 years. Based on that one experience.

But I am not 11 anymore. So why would I think the experience would be the same? I didn't give myself the opportunity to try again. I didn't give myself the opportunity to be better. I didn't give myself the opportunity to grow.

When we are able to really acknowledge how we are feeling, and face our fears, we are able to choose how to deal with whatever is challenging us.

Dream Big

I look back on my life and realise that I never really knew who I was or where I wanted to go. I was letting life just happen to me, I was not planning a life.

I now know the importance of setting goals. When you know what you want, you have the potential of making it happen. You can dream big. Life is full of choices and your potential for growth is not limited.

Don't underestimate the power of knowing who you are. We grow up inheriting other people's beliefs and we let these define us, but it doesn't have to be that way. We can create our own beliefs and we can define our own capabilities.

The thing that has helped me grow the most is getting myself several coaches and mentors, and surrounding myself with a community of like-minded people, the Queens In Business Club. I surround myself with people who inspire me, and who I can learn from. They also keep me accountable.

Life takes so many twists and turns, and it is easy to look back with regret at the opportunities I turned down because I didn't believe I was capable of achieving them.

So I want to ask you the following:
- What do you want to overcome?
- What beliefs are no longer serving you?
- What are you afraid of doing right now?

- What are you still doing that may be holding you back from the life you dream of?
- What small step can you take today to get you nearer to where you want to go?
- Who are you surrounding yourself with, and who is influencing you?
- Who do you want to keep you accountable?

We all have the resources within us to create the life we want. I believe in YOU and I have your back. Now is the right time for you to grow and live the life of your dreams.

Now is YOUR time!

About Me

I am an anxiety coach, mentor, trainer, business owner and public speaker.

Having struggled with anxiety throughout childhood and adult life, I started my business, Better Your Life, back in 2016 because I believe that no one needs to struggle with anxiety. Based on my own experience, alongside my 25+ years of coaching within the corporate world, I discovered the seven steps that anyone can use to set themselves free from anxiety and thrive.

I am a qualified practitioner in neuro linguistic programming (NLP) and neuroscience, and I am also a qualified and experienced project manager, helping you set, manage, and achieve your goals and the life you dream of.

I love being in nature and find it very calming and grounding. I enjoy open water swimming and cycling with my friends. We are crazy enough to think a 100 mile road ride is good fun!

I am the proud mum of an incredible teenager who has taught me so much. She is grounded and confident in herself, and never ceases to amaze me with what she achieves. She is the funniest person I know, and I am so grateful to her for all the joy and sunshine she brings into my life. We love spontaneous trips away, and you will often find us in a coffee shop, laughing together and catching up on our week, in whichever city or town we have decided to visit.

I want to thank my friends and my family who offer love, support, and encouragement. Thank you for always being there for me.

I also want to thank all the colleagues I have worked with previously, you helped me find my dream job!

I want to thank all my clients; past, present, and future, for letting me come on a journey with you. I feel very honoured to work with you and watch you grow.

I want to thank my mentors, Jessen James, James Nicholson, Liam Ryan and the Queens In Business Club. You inspire me, support me, and encourage me with the honest feedback I need to hear but don't necessarily want to hear!

Lastly, I would like to dedicate my chapter to my amazing girl, thank you for being you and for making me so proud. I love you with all my heart.

Be The Empress You Are

Angela Haynes-Ranger
Style Coach, Beauty Boss and Founder
Adourable

"Over the years I have learned that what is important in a dress is the woman who is wearing it" -- Yves Saint Laurent

Some of you may relate to this, but I have always known who I wanted to be from the very beginning. For as long as I can remember, I've had a passion for what I do. Not that it was in its present form, but I was always fascinated with fashion and beauty, experimenting with different styles and looks.

I also took great influence from my mum, although I didn't realise it at the time. I spent hours going through her closet trying on things and loved all the pieces she had. I eventually gave her the nickname 'Queenie' because she always reminded me of the Queen, dressed in her stylish outfits with matching hats and handbags.

To this day, that's who she's known as and it still suits her so well. Queenie was an absolute warrior, taking care of us all while working full-time as a nurse. My parents were always there and we wanted for nothing. My dad was a real provider and the sweetest, most supportive and funniest dad you could wish for. I still miss him so much.

I was the youngest of five children - I had three sisters and a brother - and we all had very different personalities. I was definitely known as the cheeky one. I knew my mind, and my direction and was always up to something whether that was roller skating every weekend (which I loved) or attending a dance class. I really enjoyed my childhood and was lucky to have the best parents ever. Whether that was allowing me to have piano lessons or attend Saturday ballet school, I was always learning something new and enjoying life.

One of my earliest memories was when my siblings had gone to school and I was at home with my mum, deciding to play 'salon'. I cut one of my pigtails thinking I could just stick it back on when I had finished. I remember approaching my mum with it in my hand and the horrified look on her face – thankfully it grew back but that look was priceless!

The passion hadn't left by the time I attended secondary school. I had the amazing opportunity for my first ever job to work as a Saturday girl at an exclusive boutique on Bond Street in London, which was full of gorgeous (and very expensive) gowns and I loved it!

Being able to help women to look and feel amazing, offering advice and ensuring they had exactly what they needed was a joy. I personally delivered gowns to The Dorchester and other prestigious hotels, conversing with those far exceeding my age and living a life not a lot of my peers had access to.

Then, in my spare time, I continued to do what I loved and what came naturally to me. I enjoyed browsing the latest collections in Topshop , Oxford Circus, or on Carnaby Street soaking up the vibes and looking for new inspiration. I became the 'go to' person for styling with friends as well as family. I even managed to persuade one of my teachers to allow me to French braid her hair most lessons while she taught the class! I loved the process of transitioning someone from look A to look B. I spent a lot of time hiding the latest colour I'd decided to dye my hair from my mum, whether that be brown, red or on one occasion, blue!

After sitting my final exams, my best friend and I decided to travel around Europe for a month in summer. OMG what a trip! First to Paris, then Germany, Switzerland, and finally, Rome. I was totally ecstatic. I found European women so stylish and put together. I made connections with a lot of the designers there and fell in love with fashion all over again. The majority of the money I had with me was spent on clothes, shoes, bags and accessories.

Back from our trip, I received so many compliments and questions on the pieces that I had brought home: "Wow that's lovely Angie – can you get one for me?" or "Angie, can I borrow that?"

It was actually a comment that a friend made at that time which gave me my first lightbulb moment for business. She said: "It's about time you started charging for all your advice and services."

"Hmmm," I thought… "maybe."

Upping My Game

I always wanted to be an entrepreneur. Looking around, I could see that most people, even though they had worked hard all their lives, either really struggled to make ends meet, working in between jobs, or had careers they hated. I definitely knew I didn't want to be in either one of those camps. I knew I had to make it happen no matter what, but as we all know, sometimes life has other plans and the road can end up being a winding one.

I decided I was going to do what made me happy and that was that. I wanted to attend the London College of Fashion. I set my heart on getting in, studied hard to get the grades, attended my interview - more with excitement than nerves, and was over the moon to be accepted. I don't know what I would have done if I wasn't accepted because there was no Plan B.

I'm so glad my parents didn't pressure me to go to university at that time. They were always supportive of me and could see that this was what I really wanted to do. Studying a fashion and beauty course on one of the most famous shopping streets in London - I'd call that a result!

My three years there were amazing and everything I had hoped for. On graduating, I landed a job straight away in a prestigious store on Regent Street. And within six months, I was asked to help run the new salon on Oxford Street along with my manager.

She was a great manager. I loved how supportive she was, as well as her kind and empathetic nature. She is someone who I will never forget as she gave me the confidence to really stand in my own abilities and was instrumental in my growth back then.

Unfortunately, after only a few months together, she had to suddenly return to Australia for family reasons and things were never quite the same. But I loved my job and I loved the women I was honoured to help. Being able to hear about their lives, goals and aspirations, as well as their troubles, perceived limitations, and their lack of confidence really struck a chord.

"But you're amazing!" I'd say. "How many people could go through all that and still keep going?" It was something I heard myself saying more and more often. I was just glad to be able to give them an hour or two of escapism, make them look and feel amazing, and spread a little happiness and sparkle over them before they left.

It didn't take me long to come to the conclusion that WOMEN ARE INCREDIBLE!

I knew without a doubt that one day I wanted to have my own business and work with incredible women just like the ones I was working with every day. Although I enjoyed my job, I wanted to be in a position to do more. I wanted to `up my game' and felt I needed to gain more experience. I needed to keep growing if I was going to run a successful business one day.

I decided that I'd love to work with one of the most prestigious cosmetics brands around, Estee Lauder. I plucked up the courage to call them and was excited to be invited for an interview. I couldn't believe it when they offered me my own account in Kensington! I did so well there that after just one month, I was asked to join the team at Harrods.

Working in that environment was a real eye opener. You get to meet so many people from around the world. I also went on to manage a boutique for the company in Selfridges. I began to realise that no matter who you are, where you're from, what background you have, whether you're a celebrity or a woman next door, ALL of us experience self-doubt. We ALL experience a lack of confidence at times and we often play smaller than our full potential.

So I asked myself a question: why don't we trust ourselves?

As my skills and experience grew, I was promoted from Account Manager to Special Events Coordinator and I was over the moon! Anyone who knows me, knows I love a good party and being able to connect with people. I was able to organise a host of different events for women from makeup workshops to collaborating on photoshoots with fashion magazines and brands. Apart from totally being in my element, I knew I was growing, progressing and things were going to plan. I loved my life!

Am I Losing Myself?

By this time, I had been in a relationship and had my two beautiful daughters. Relationships were important to me. My mum and dad were married for 55 years up until he passed away and I loved the stability I had throughout my life. It was something I knew I wanted for my children.

I was doing well, happy in life and happy at work, but noticed that I wasn't being supported. I began to feel anger and resentment from my partner. Wasn't it a good thing that I had, more or less, achieved the goals I had set for myself so far? Isn't your partner meant to encourage and support you?

I was finding it more and more difficult to juggle home life with raising a family, especially with the increasing hostility. Early mornings, late nights, and some weekends were not a good recipe for family life. My parents were amazing as always, stepping in as daily childcare. I wouldn't have lasted so long if it hadn't been for them. At least when I was working I never had to worry as I knew the girls were in perfect hands.

It was my mum who said to me one day: "You can't carry on like this, you're wearing yourself out. You need to take some time out." I knew she was right but I loved my job so much and had worked hard for it. I knew what my long-term vision was and felt as though this was the best way to achieve it. I wanted to be more present for the family but it was an emotional struggle. I eventually made the decision to leave the role and took some time out to concentrate more on my family.

I knew I needed a role which was more structured in regards to my time. I've always had an interest in law. I had a thing for justice and fighting for the underdog, I decided to undertake some additional training and worked at a local law firm near home.

It was only a short walk away from where I lived which made things a lot easier at home. I remember everyone was a bit scared of the Senior Partner – but not me. He had been the one to interview me, so when he gave it out, I gave it right back along with a cheeky smile and he seemed to respect me for that.

I found everyone at the practice really supportive, apart from the female solicitor I was working for - she was awful. I always had the belief that women helped women but she definitely didn't get that memo. I promised myself I was never going to be like that.

At that time, I also had to complete my business and law degree. It wasn't easy working as well as studying but I felt I had no choice. I'd regularly have to study until 3am in the morning, waking again at 6am to start the day. I did that for two years and it wasn't easy at all but I did it.

I was working primarily with cases affecting women. Some of the scenarios were heart breaking. I knew I could help them if they had been my own personal clients. I could help build their confidence, change their mindset and primarily take back control of their lives. That passion for helping women, instilling self-love and building their confidence was reignited but in a deeper, more meaningful way.

Deeper And Deeper Into A Black Hole

My dad had suddenly been taken ill. My days consisted of working in the office, juggling clients, then spending time at the hospital before going home. We also did shifts in looking after my mum. She'd never been alone. She'd always had my dad there.

To say I was mentally and physically exhausted was an understatement. I was constantly rushing around, I was losing my focus. Then one morning, everything changed. It was around 5am when I received a call from my partner to say that he had been on his way to work and had had an accident on the M25. He said he was OK and that the paramedics were there. They were taking him to the hospital. I was about to ask where but he ended the call.

I just stood there, the phone still in my hand, wondering why he had ended the call so abruptly. I was starting to worry when he called again and repeated the same conversation... I was confused. Didn't he remember that he had already called to say that? Panic started to set in. I asked to speak to the paramedic and they explained he was OK, they were just taking him to get checked out at the hospital. He was released later that day and everything seemed OK... Or so we thought.

The accident really had an impact on me. We never really know what's round the corner do we? I was always a go-getter and this made me question where I was in life. I made a decision to start taking action towards my goals again and to get back on track.

I began speaking to people about what I was doing. I started attending networking events to connect with like-minded women. Although I had continued working low-key with clients, this time I was more intentional, it was more than just about beauty and styling, it was deeper than that. It was about looking good and feeling great in your confidence as well as in your purpose.

The referrals came in and I started working with some great clients. I felt so much more on point and the level of service was more intimate and bespoke. On reflection, this taught me that you should never disregard your experiences. I believe they are there to help you grow as well as teach you lessons. All experiences are valuable and they all have a part to play in your progression and your growth. It's how you choose to use them which will either help you or hinder you.

In my case, even though I had taken a detour on a totally different path (I feel that fashion, beauty and law are so polar opposites), the experiences and skills I have gained from both have been invaluable in helping me to serve the women I do today in a way that I'm so grateful and blessed to do.

It Doesn't Get Easier, You Just Get Stronger

Things were going well. I was building something I was proud of and it was an exciting time seeing things coming together. All the years of ideas actually coming to fruition and successfully too. Being able to work with women, see the transformation, not just physically but mentally, was the best feeling ever.

Things at home had settled down a bit too. I was organising events as well as working one-to-one with clients. I was happy with how things were progressing. I had a long way to go to accomplish the vision but I'd started which was the most important thing and the response was amazing.

At the same time, my partner was still in a lot of pain from the accident. I kept saying he needed to get himself checked out but he didn't. Months went by and the pain just got worse. Eventually, after a few appointments and after insisting on tests being done, he was sent to the hospital. I remember the consultant looking at us both from across his desk when he said: "It's cancer."

I heard him say, "We're going to have to operate quickly, it's quite advanced. The nurse will speak with you and give you some support to tell the children." To be honest, I heard the words and I knew what they meant and they landed hard. I heard my partner respond, "I don't want to tell them." I don't know if this was to protect him or to protect them. I was numb.

This really can't be happening...

The next few months were a haze and basically consisted of hospital visits. My bubble of positivity and hope had burst. I was conflicted, I felt I was living a lie. I was forced into living a lie. I was angry, really angry. I felt trapped in my own emotions. It's not surprising that things took a downward spiral. My partner became angry at everything. I felt, at times, that I couldn't breathe from all the anxiety. My health was being impacted. I lost my dad soon after. My relationship broke down. I decided to go it alone and turned all my focus to the girls.

Things progressively got worse and the cancer spread. He was a different person to the one I had previously known. Dealing with the abuse and the coercive control was the hardest thing I'd ever been through but by the grace of God I did. He passed away in the summer of 2020. The mental challenges on us were huge. We all went through our own individual grief but we were close and we had each other. I'm so proud of that.

I hadn't come this far to lose my way now. I knew I had to fight. I knew I had to take all the challenges and somehow turn them into something positive and I had to believe that I could.

Even though I'd experienced all of this, I knew my worth. I knew the life I wanted. I knew what me and my daughters deserved.

But how was I going to get back? I had so much brain fog. I felt confused, numb and unable to focus. How was I ever going to get back to me? Who even was I anymore? I knew I had to hold on to the essence of me... that's what would get me through.

So I came up with a plan.

I worked on my mindset.
I set a daily routine.
I exercised and had a healthier diet.
I chose an outfit and got dressed every day.
I did my hair, my makeup and pampered myself more.
I started reading again.
I listened to music.

In essence, I poured into me. I started setting goals – nothing too big, just small goals initially.

Then, because I looked better, I felt better. And because I felt better, I started showing up more.

Getting My Mojo Back
Little did I know I was about to level up both in my business and in my personal life.

I was asked to be a speaker for International Women's Day with a UK company that was hosting an event in Antigua. Wow! The two things I love the most – travel and helping women. And in the Caribbean too! But how could I? What would I deliver? The doubts and fear came rushing in again.

"Of course you can," my daughters reassured me. "Go!" I knew it was time to step out of my comfort zone. If I really wanted to level up then this was my chance. So I ignored the fear, confirmed my place and started preparing. I was both excited and scared. I was going to do this and more importantly, enjoy the opportunity I'd been given. In that moment, I felt the old me coming back.

Those few days in Antigua were amazing. Our host had arranged for us to stay in a private luxury villa overlooking the sea and it was just what I needed. I made some really good friends on that trip. The event was for business owners and was held over two days at a beautiful hotel in the bay. This was just the push I needed. It forced me to start thinking about business again and to create a presentation that would both serve and lead to new international connections and business clients.

The room was full and my session was greatly received. I was buzzing after all the positive feedback. We were invited onto one of the radio shows to discuss the event and talk about our businesses. We even had the privilege of being invited to meet the Governor-General of Antigua and Barbuda and his wife to discuss the event. They wanted to find out more about our businesses which was a once in a lifetime experience.

All of this growth just from believing in myself and taking action. I think there's a huge lesson there. My experiences have made me stronger, more resilient and more comfortable in my own skin.

If there's any advice I would give to you, it would have to be:

1. NEVER GIVE UP! I wouldn't have gotten here without the challenges and I'm thankful for the lessons learnt.
2. Learn to trust your instinct. It's there for a reason.
3. There's more than one path to a destination – just keep moving.
4. Be coachable – it's a great way to achieve personal growth.
5. Find good mentors. Learn from people who are successful and have done it before you… That's priceless.
6. Find your community. It is VITAL to surround yourself with like-minded people. The Queens In Business Club has played a MASSIVE part in my growth. Being in business can be a lonely place so surround yourself with supporters.
7. DON'T PLAY SMALL! Go all out and BELIEVE in yourself.

Through my journey, I believe that the strongest actions for you to take is to love yourself, be yourself and shine amongst those who never believed you could. Believe that YOU are your greatest gift.

And now I am happy to say, here I am at a place in my life where it's my goals, my dreams, my decisions, my way.

About Me

I'm a style coach, beauty boss and entrepreneur who likes to have fun!

I was born and raised in London in a crazy family and am the youngest of five children. I have two beautiful daughters, and absolutely love to travel.

I have always had a passion for what I do and I think the most beautiful thing that a woman can wear is her confidence. As the Founder of Adourable, a place where we help you to elevate your style, glow in your beauty and step into your greatness , I want to empower you to feel bold, brave and beautiful in your own skin. I want you to be able to embrace your unique style and never be afraid to express yourself.

As women, we have the power to change the world. Your personal brand helps you to show up confidently for yourself whilst making your mark in business and your career as well as in your personal life.

My goal is to help you with the way you see yourself so that you always feel confident and assured no matter where life takes you. I truly believe that when you look good, you feel good, and when you feel good you *do* good. So let's start the journey!

My mission is to help women to find their most authentic self and start showing up as Her. I can't wait to see you thrive and shine!

I would like to dedicate this chapter to my mum Queenie, one of the most inspiring women I know and to my beautiful girls Lauren and Ashleigh. I would not have gotten here without you. Your love, support, understanding and beautiful light lets me know I am truly, truly blessed. And finally, to all the amazing women out there - those I have already met and those I am yet to meet - believe in yourself and believe in what you can do. And most importantly of all, don't forget to be the empress you were born to be!

Discovering Your Potential Will Never Go Out Of Style

Dr. Theodora Thomadaki (BSc., MA, PhD, FHEA)
Specialist in women's makeover culture, lifestyle media and psychoanalysis

"The women whom I love and admire for their strength and grace did not get that way because sh*t worked out. They got that way because sh*t went wrong, and they handled it"
-- Elizabeth Gilbert

During the school year of 2000/2001, in a charming Greek city called Thessaloniki my mother, Evangelia, was invited to pay a visit to my high school to learn about my progress. I purposely hid behind the classroom door, anxiously waiting to hear what my teacher had to say. I don't recall much of what was discussed but I do remember the following statement from my teacher, word for word:

"I am sorry Mrs. Thomadaki, but Theodora does not have the academic capacity to progress into higher education, and to be brutally honest, there is no chance in a million that she will make it to university."

My name is Dr. Theodora Thomadaki, and I am an academic scholar and expert in women's makeover culture, lifestyle media, post feminism and psychoanalysis. From a young age and throughout school, I found myself always struggling with reading and writing. I would be in awe of my peers, teachers and people who could study and achieve high grades so effortlessly. Reading books was such a difficult task for me and I could spend hours and hours per day just to make sense of a few pages.

I always felt the pressure to keep up and compare myself with what others could achieve in school and that strained myself emotionally and had an impact on my self-confidence. Throughout high school, the teachers' view of me was unanimous - I was not considered the cleverest of the bunch. I was often described as a kind, polite and a very sensitive girl. My sensitivity has always been perceived as a weakness (although I now consider it my biggest strength).

I do remember being highly driven though, and wanting to stand out from the crowd, to prove to myself (and to others) that I am good enough, and that I have something valuable to offer as a person. But I did not know what was special about me nor how to unravel my string of potential.

Meeting Failure On The Way To Success
As I reached the final year of high school, the dreaded exams were slowly approaching. My parents hired personal tutors to help me in preparation for the assessments. I studied tirelessly from day until night, and I put all my effort into winning my teachers' praise by proving that they were wrong about me.

A few days before the exam period was about to commence, I took a little break from studying and turned on my TV. I settled on this day time Greek show, where coincidentally, my school teacher was being interviewed. They wanted to delve into how she successfully obtained her PhD.

The interviewer asked her, "What does it take to earn a PhD?" Her response was exactly what I was expecting to hear: "Outstanding grades in all subjects from school, all the way up to university; excellent study skills and a lot of time spent reading books."

I immediately told myself, Theodora you will never get a PhD, this will never be you. I had fully internalised my teacher's principles as the norm - that excelling in school is the only possible route to success.

By July 2001, I had completed all of my final exams and felt confident that I did well. But reality hit hard when I received my grades. The mark was just enough to let me graduate from high school, but not enough for me to qualify for university. I had proved my teachers right about me. I locked myself into my room and cried for hours.

I felt lost and defeated. I had let my parents down. Friends and relatives would ask me how I did with my exams and when I told them, their response was: "Well, you probably didn't study hard enough. You should try harder." My heart broke immediately, and tears welled up in my eyes.

As I contemplated my not so bright future in my room, my parents came to chat to me about what I would like to do next. I told them that I felt so lost and that I had no idea where to go or what to do next. Always so wonderful and supportive, they came up with a proposition:

"We believe in you, Theodora and you have lots of potential. School exams do not define your character, personality, and self-worth. You have two choices. You can either spend another year here to retake the exams *or* you can travel abroad, start afresh and take your time to discover what you are passionate about."

I was intrigued. I knew that I did not want to go through the same demoralising experience of retaking the school exams. So I thought about the latter option to travel abroad and restart anew.

At that time, my sister Evangelia (my inspiration) - who had been living in London for two years - had just arrived in Greece for the summer holidays. Seeing me so lost, she declared, "You have got to come to London with me. We will have an amazing time living together. I will support you and help you get back on your feet. We can invite friends over for dinner, go to parties, and go shopping! And the best part is, we can come home any time we want to."

Going to London to start afresh with my sister by my side, and the option to return home whenever I wanted to, made me feel secure and excited. But there was just one big obstacle - I could not speak a single word of English.

Although I was terrified, I decided to take a leap of faith and flew to London with the purpose of rediscovering myself and my true potential.

Strength Lies In The Ability To Start Over

It was September 2001 when I moved to London. I needed to start right from the beginning and learn my ABCs in a new language, so I enrolled in a college to study English. And when I completed that, a year later, I made the bold move to apply for A Levels to gain the credits I needed to enter university.

The college panel advised me that I needed at least two more years of English lessons before I was ready to enter A Levels. But I felt so driven and motivated to make progress that I came up with a proposition for them: permit me A Level entry so I can attend the classes as an observer instead. I explained that I wanted to maximise my learning experience of the British educational system. I wanted to learn how these courses are delivered, so I can prepare myself for the future by knowing what to expect.

I assured the committee that I was ready to accept full responsibility if I didn't pass my exams and that I would be happy to retake the year if I needed to. I managed to convince the panel, but they had one condition. I needed to directly speak to the teachers, explain my circumstances and receive permission from them to join their classes. I felt I had nothing to lose and plenty to gain from this experience.

When Monday morning came around, my very first class was psychology. I waited outside and as students were entering the room, I greeted my psychology teacher. She looked so strict that it made me weak to my knees, but I built the courage to explain my story:

"I am aware that my English is not at an advanced level, but I want to test my abilities and see how far I can go. Please allow me this opportunity to join your class. I am more than happy to sit at the back of the room."

She looked me straight in the eyes and in all seriousness, said, "I can see it in your eyes. You are driven, motivated and passionate to achieve. I am not going to get in your way, nor stop you. It may be challenging, but something tells me that you are ready for this. I would be delighted for you to join my class and please, sit with the rest of the students."

I was over the moon! From then on, I made sure I was always on time and did not miss a single class. But it was tough. I struggled catching up with all the new reading materials as I had to translate textbook pages to Greek first, learn any new vocabulary, then study the reading back in English. So, to learn two pages of reading materials would take around three days to complete. But I did not care. I kept on going as I was enjoying the knowledge I was gaining.

After two months of lessons, I had submitted written coursework and my psychology teacher asked me for a talk in private. I felt sick to my stomach. Would she ask me to leave the class? Am I not good enough to continue?

To my surprise, she said, "Your hard work and dedication to your studies is impressive and I am proud of you, but are you aware that you are dyslexic?"

I responded, "Does this mean I am not smart enough to get into the university?"

She was mortified by my response. "Theodora, there is nothing that can get in the way of you achieving your goals, except you. When one is passionate and driven about their goals and is willing to put in the hard work, despite setbacks, then they are bound for success. Being dyslexic does not mean you are not smart; you only need some guidance and support with your studies."

Even though I did not fully understand what dyslexia meant at the time, I immediately took on board all the advice and support made available by my college. Gradually, everything started to shift. They encouraged me to explore a learning style that would fit my needs better. It made studying far more fun, effortless and productive than it had ever been before.

Two years later, I successfully completed my A Level exams and was even awarded for my hard work, dedication, and outstanding grades. Shortly after, I received a letter of acceptance to study BSc in psychology at the University of Surrey, Roehampton, but I did not stop there.

I completed my MA in psychoanalytic studies from The Tavistock and Portman NHS Foundation Trust, and a PhD in cultural studies at the University of Roehampton, which awarded me the title of Doctor of Philosophy.

It Always Seems Impossible Until It Is Done
My decision to do a PhD was prompted by my psychoanalytic studies under the Tavistock Clinic, where I trained in infant observation. It is here that I developed a strong passion for the field of psychoanalysis. I was interested in how we could better understand society, our sense of identity and emotional experiences in contemporary culture.

In 2009, I successfully completed my MA on how the characters of 'Sex and the City' offer everyday women a space for female and emotional relatedness on topics such as sex, relationships, and friendships. I wanted to take this idea further, extending to popular media, celebrities and makeover culture and how they can provide positive opportunities for women to attain self-confidence and emotional awareness.

To complete a PhD, I had to make two important decisions. Firstly, to find the gap in the market and develop an innovative research proposal on a topic that will have cultural impact in academia and beyond. Secondly, I had to be passionate and become the best representative of my work.

Because when you embark on a big new project you must believe in it and love it otherwise, no one will buy into it.

Outside my scholarly work, I turn to fashion, accessories, and make-up to explore and express my feminine identity, which boosts my confidence and makes me feel more dynamic in my daily life.

So when I started researching lifestyle media and makeover culture, I took a closer look at how celebrity culture and media have negatively impacted women's body image and self-confidence by simply depicting fashionably airbrushed and unrealistic female bodies as an indicator of ideal beauty.

In all this negativity, I was looking for the positive solution that could potentially restore some of this emotional damage and showcase a way of supporting women to play with fashion, make-up, and clothing in a creative way and as a means to rediscover their identity and voice their authentic personality.

One late night, as I was laying 'on the couch' (a popular term to indicate psychoanalysis), surfing through TV channels, I came across a new makeover series called 'How to Look Good Naked'. As I watched, I observed how Gok Wan's fashion knowledge was being utilised to help women gain self and body-confidence through emotional awareness and self-reflective practices. If I could research the potential therapeutic value of Gok Wan's makeover series from a psychoanalytic lens, I would have the perfect foundation for my PhD. What was amazing for me was that no one had ever looked into this before. I had found the gap in the market.

I started my PhD in 2010 and working on it was not an easy task. I felt I was training for a marathon but with no finish line in sight. In my journey, many doubted the potential of my work, telling me that my PhD on makeover culture was not important and had no value. But I would always respond with a cheeky smile: "Wait and you will see!" I was passionate about my research and was truly convinced that it would have a great impact on audiences way beyond academia.

In 2017, through hard work, endless tears and absolute emotional and mental exhaustion, my 450 page PhD book successfully proved that Gok Wan's makeover series did indeed provide a culturally 'therapeutic' media environment in helping women to make sense of their body insecurities. By using fashion practices and stylistic techniques, Gok Wan generated self-reflective opportunities for ordinary women, giving them the space for emotional growth by simply voicing and acknowledging their struggles - something that usually remained hidden, neglected and culturally unacknowledged at the time.

Drawing on my research, I published academic articles for the journal of Free Associations and Clothing Cultures, and received the Psychology of Women Section (POWS) Prize Shortlist Award in recognition of outstanding feminist work in postgraduate psychology. I was also appointed a Founding Scholar of the British Psychoanalytic Council for my significant contribution to the advancement of psychoanalytic thinking, and I was invited to become a member of British Psychoanalytic Council Scholars Committee and Editor-in-Chief of their newsletter.

I was so proud of myself. But I wanted to reach more women and help them find their confidence. So I put my PR skills into practise and managed to attract the attention of the fashion consultant himself - Gok Wan!

Then in 2019, I invited him to be interviewed at a one-day event that I was organising to bring together scholars and practitioners working in fashion, lifestyle media and PR. During his interview, a member of the audience asked Gok Wan how he felt about me writing my doctoral research on him and his makeover series. To my surprise, he took my PhD book out of his bag and showed the audience, holding it like it was a trophy! He said, "Theodora, you have taken something that a lot of people frown upon and think is unnecessary, and you have made it really important. I know it has changed people's lives already."

Having Gok Wan recognise the value of my work in such a beautiful way was the biggest sense of accomplishment that I have ever experienced. His opinion mattered to me and it was that moment that I experienced my own 'How To Look Good Naked' moment next to him. I could finally see the potential of what I had achieved and what I am capable of achieving with my passion and determination.

As a result of the social media publicity and press attention that my interview received, I was invited to deliver talks about my research to students and audiences in the field of fashion, media and beauty. A fire was lit within me and I wanted to do more than just teach students. I had a new-found entrepreneurial enthusiasm and wanted to collaborate between academia, media and the creative industries.

I started by organising events at the university with industry experts and professionals from the fields of journalism, PR, television, photography, digital media and film. While my industry networking connections were growing fast, I took initiative and delivered talks and seminars on the value of emotional intelligence in business and the importance of emotional awareness in developing business strategies. It was important to showcase why emotions play a part in business decision making. I also mentored students who often lack self-confidence and were oblivious of their talents to motivate them. I helped them build their confidence and recognise their own potential.

In October 2021, Sunna Coleman (Blogging for Business Coach and Co-Founder of Queens In Business Club) invited me to deliver a guest session for the Club's members on the value of emotional intelligence in business. I then went on to receive the greatest honour of being interviewed alongside Gok Wan for the first Queens In Business Magazine on the topic of 'Empower Dressing' where I discussed how women can play with fashion in a creative way to reflect their authentic identities and increase confidence. Because confidence is not in the body, it is in our positive mindset of how we show up for ourselves and for the world.

Emotional and self-awareness are an important part of our personal, business, and social lives. By being aware of our own emotions, we can gain clarity of how we communicate with others as well as how honest we are with ourselves. Looking inwards into our emotional world, with no self-judgment but with love, kindness and understanding towards our strengths and vulnerabilities, we can achieve emotional growth and maturity.

Society tends to see women in business who are in touch with their emotions as weak. I often get annoyed listening to statements such as: "There is no emotion in business." I am sorry, but there is!

Emotional awareness leads to the development of emotional intelligence, which in the entrepreneurial world translates into confidence, resilience, adaptability, individuality, reinvention, and growth. Tapping into your emotions is one of the best business deals you can make with yourself.

I Am Strong. I Am Enough.

For the past ten years, I have been teaching at the university, have published several academic papers, and have received numerous awards. I have collaborated with other scholars, and stretched myself above and beyond to prove that I am worthy of a permanent contract. I was trying to remain patient and was waiting for the right timing, but the stress and anxiety were building as the yearly contracts were renewed last minute.

But in the last year or so, I felt very unsettled and I started to not enjoy teaching as much as I used to. I had a niggling feeling that the new academic term in September would be challenging. I tried not to think too much about it and put it out of my mind.

Then, in October 2021, I met up with Sunna Coleman and she gave me a copy of the Queen's In Business book, Time to Reign.

When I returned home, I poured myself a lovely drink and started reading the first chapter 'Your Life, Your Empire, Your Rules' written by the wonderful Chloë Bisson (Co-Founder of Queens In Business Club). After reading a couple of pages, I paused and started feeling very anxious. Chloë's chapter speaks about her four years of hard work at the company she was working for and how much of herself she invested to build it. But that all came crashing down one day when she was told by her boss that they will need to let her go. Reading her chapter, I had a premonition that something similar was coming my way very soon.

That very Monday, I found out that my contract would soon come to an end. I cried all the way home. I felt the same numbness that Chloë described so accurately in her chapter.

Everything fell apart inside me. I felt like my passion and determination for what I was doing, my genuine care to support students to find their career potential was not enough nor recognised. Working overtime, plus weekends, never taking annual leave, going above and beyond myself to prove my worth was completely disregarded and not appreciated.

I immediately took matters into my own hands and looked for another job. As I began sending off my job applications, I started to receive invites to job interviews on a weekly basis, but they were not successful. My family and friends told me that what is meant for me will come my way. I wanted to believe them, but I fell into the trap of self-deprecating thoughts that made me feel defeated.

One night, as I was scrolling through social media feeling upset, I read the following: "Having a rough day? Place your hand over your heart. Feel that? That's called purpose... Don't give up!" I realised there and then that I needed to stop putting myself down and start being positive and trust my abilities. The following day, I received a job interview invite.

On the morning of my interview, I woke up feeling emotionally drained, but I tried my best to remain positive and build up my self-confidence. I stowed away all my negative thoughts, put on my favourite dress and applied my best make up as if I was going out to meet friends.

After my online interview ended, I sat in front of my computer screen filled with unsettled emotions. So I went for a walk to clear my mind. As I left my house, for the first time in ages (I had been hiding away since the news of my contract terminating), the sky looked so majestically pink that it took my breath away and made me feel at peace.

Five minutes later, I received an email announcing that I got the job! For the first time in my life, I loudly said to myself, "I am so proud of you, Theodora! Girl, you've done it again!"

As this chapter now comes to a close (metaphorically and literally) and I am now opening a new one in my life, I am determined to stop focusing on what I haven't achieved or what I was not successful at. For too long I have relied on family, friends, teachers, colleagues and sometimes my own students to boost my confidence and remind me of my accomplishments, my charisma and that I am simply good enough.

But the person I most wanted to hear those words from was my own self, and I can finally say I have accomplished that.

Now that I feel strong, I am working towards being able to support more women like myself who struggle with self-doubt. Through public speaking, social media, and features, I want to help more women realise their full potential and understand their emotions so that they can succeed in their own chosen paths.

So, my advice to women in business who want a little push of confidence to follow their dreams is to stay true to your values and beliefs, open up about your struggles with a supportive network of women like the Queen In Business Club, who will listen to you and give you a safe space for meaningful conversation.

In our daily business lives, we have endless spreadsheets for everything - money coming in or out, lists of clients, diaries, deadlines, goals, and objectives and so on. But what about your emotional growth within your business? You are the greatest asset of your business and your biggest investment.

Start your growth by writing a reflective journal and make entry notes on your feelings and emotions when you have a great day or an uneasy one. Express how you feel about your strengths and vulnerabilities but make sure to tell your inner critic to 'zip the lip'.

Emotionally reflect on the decision you want to make. Above all, believe in yourself, acknowledge and appreciate your emotions, and embrace self-awareness. In this way, your challenges become your growth and your success story.

About Me

I am an award winning academic, dynamic public speaker and mentor, with an entrepreneurial spirit and a commitment to empower women in self-doubt to realise their own potential and make sense of their emotional experiences.

Having successfully demonstrated in my PhD the therapeutic value of Gok Wan's fashion makeover series 'How To Look Good Naked (Channel 4, 2006-2010), I am an expert in women's emotional experience in makeover culture, lifestyle media and psychoanalysis.

I have given countless talks and seminars on my research and published two academic papers: 'Gok Wan On The Couch' (Free Associations, 2017) and 'Getting Naked With Gok Wan' (Clothing Cultures, 2020). For my significant contribution to the advancement of psychoanalytic thinking to academia and beyond, I was appointed a Founder Scholar of the British Psychoanalytic Council.

In 2021, I was nominated as a finalist in the Best Supporter category at the Queens In Business Awards. Drawing on my experiences I hope to create media opportunities through talks, events, social media, where I can inspire women to achieve emotional awareness and strengthen their emotional intelligence as this will help them to stay motivated, maintain a positive attitude and utilise their leadership skills by simply being true to themselves.

I dedicate my chapter to my parents Angelo and Evangelia, my sister Evangelia, my niece Christina, and all my friends who are a force to be reckoned with - especially to Julie, Samantha and the 'Fab Six' who empower me to stay positive, trust the process and believe in myself.

Finally, to all the powerful women out there who work hard to achieve their dreams, who shed tears on their pillows at night, but are still finding the courage to get up and keep going - you are all superheroes and I salute you!

Problems Seed Opportunities

Ousha Demello
Inspirational Business Trainer and International
Public Speaker
The Uplift Academy

"Don't quit. Suffer now and live the rest of your life as a champion" -- Muhammad Ali

Have you ever been told that you have to study and work hard to be successful?

That belief was ingrained in me after being in the education industry. The first time I ever felt like I had a nice long break was after the delivery of my daughter, Ellsa, when I was on maternity leave. But as it came to an end, it was time for me to resume work on a full-time basis.

Being at work felt different this time.

I was restless thinking about Ellsa, how she cried when I dropped her at her nursery. My mind and body were tired but I kept myself focused, knowing my students needed me. I came home brain dead most nights. I could not even speak to my husband. My daughter hardly slept at night either, which kept me awake.

Due to tiredness and exposure in the nursery, Ellsa constantly caught a cold, making me and my husband ill too. It all became exhausting. Nevertheless, we continued to give 100% at work. But although we were working so hard, our bank

122

balance was always minus at the end of the month. I wondered what we were working for!

Eventually, I decided that this was not the way I wanted to continue living. I could not stop wondering how other parents managed to go back to their full-time jobs while being parents. Kids require time, and I did not understand how parents are expected to do everything as usual! My daughter was so tiny and yet already tied up in a stressful life, always being rushed around and feeling tired. It was not right for her to live this way.

I realised that I needed to make a change. I decided that I wanted to have more freedom and more time with my daughter. And when Ellsa turned 15 months old, my husband and I decided it may be the right time to have another baby, I became even more motivated to start my own business. But I knew I could not do it alone.

Therefore, I invested in professional training and mentorship. That's when I met Jessen James. He was able to fast-track my progress and gave me clarity. I knew exactly what I had to do to get to where I wanted to be. A year later, my dream of working with Chloë Bisson came true, and I joined the Queen In Business Club.

Growth Has No Deadline

I have always had a growth mindset and often take on challenges that help me develop my skills and enhance my knowledge. When I was setting up my business, I knew I had so much more to offer to the world. Nonetheless, with a busy career and family to take care of, I carried on in autopilot mode. In the back of my mind, I was anxious that it was getting too late to start my own business.

The reality is that it is never too late to do anything in life that will elevate you. Growth has no deadline! You have probably heard of the proverb, "The best time to plant a tree was 20 years ago, the second best time is now."

One thing that was certain for me was that I did not want to waste any more time. February 14th, 2020, I found out that I was pregnant. My husband and I were over the moon. This gave me more drive to start my business as soon as possible. My gut feeling kept on telling me it was time to level up - there is so much more to this life.

Successful people always look at ways to do better. People are different, and what works for one may not work for another. Success and growth are things that you need to define for yourself and it's important to be in the right mindset.

Here are three simple ways you can switch to a growth mindset:

1. Change your language and use positive affirmations every day.
2. Visualise where you want to be. How will you feel when you achieve your goals? Then visualise how you will feel if you don't achieve your goals.

3. Don't let fear be an obstacle. You can either fear everything and run or face everything and rise.

Armed with a growth mindset and buzzing with excitement after training with Jessen James, I was ready to kick start my business journey. I had a clear vision and started planning my goals. I was still working a full-time job and had a busy household, but I was excited and I persevered.

Then Covid hit!

Life got busier than ever. I had to teach from home, and it was unfortunate that Ellsa's nursery was also closed. Suddenly, I had to adapt and learn new software that I had never used before so we could teach remotely. I needed to make sure I supported my students, not just for their business course, but also to ensure they were coping well with all the changes.

At the same time, Ellsa was only two years old and needed a lot of attention. Add in the pregnancy, I was feeling overwhelmed and stressed, and the pressure became too much. I had a nervous breakdown. During the first week of Easter break, April 2020, I had to be hospitalised with severe stomach pain, only to find out that we had lost our baby at twelve weeks. I felt sad, demotivated and lost.

Around a month later, while tidying up my office, I came across my written goals. This motivated me to start looking at what I had previously planned and pick up where I had left off. This was a welcome distraction from what had happened to me. I set some new goals for myself and started working on them one by one.

I realised that it all starts with a positive mindset and having the desire to grow. Goals are informed actions. To move forward towards your definition of growth, you will need to take some actions. If you want growth and success in your life or in your business, it is important that you set some clear goals. If I had not set my goals beforehand, I believe I probably would not have carried on pursuing them.

No matter what situation you may be in, it is never too late to set new goals, reorganise, refocus, or make new plans that you wish to accomplish. By setting goals, you will be able to get back on track and push yourself forward.

But your definition of growth has to be clear. Having clear goals is like having a standard by which you can measure your progress and understand the results you have achieved better.

Here is a simple method for how you can set measurable goals:

1. Write down your goals.
2. Set a benchmark.
3. For each benchmark, set a milestone.
4. For each milestone set the actions required.

Take one step at a time and keep on moving forward. Growth and happiness are found along the way, not at the end of the road. When you set your goals, it is not simply about the results, it is about the lessons and experiences you learn along the way. Life is always going to change, so will your goals and plans.

Falling Down Is An Accident, Staying Down Is A Choice
Two months later, after I started picking myself up and working on my business, I was pleasantly surprised to find out that I was pregnant again. I was over the moon.

In July 2020, we moved to a bigger house, and everything was very exciting.

By August, when I had my 12 weeks scan, I was sadly told that there was no heartbeat.

I could not believe this was happening again. I felt emotionally drained and felt like giving up on everything I was doing, including the progress I had made in my business start-up.

Life is full of adversity. Some people stay calm in the moments and some crumble. Two weeks later, I was due to attend another training session. Despite feeling down and demotivated, I really pushed myself to attend. I felt very fragile but I wanted to show up. Being in a positive and progressive surrounding helped me pick myself up again and focus on my goals once more.

Whatever you have been through or are going through, remember that you are responsible for your own happiness. Many people rely on other people or external factors to determine their path, and as a result, they feel powerless and lacking control.

On the other hand, resilient people take full responsibility and control of their lives. It does not mean that you must do this alone, but it is imperative that you hold yourself accountable for your life, growth, success, and happiness. That way, when you get knocked down, you will be able to bounce forward, not backwards.

In November 2020, for the third time that year, I was fortunate to fall pregnant again. This time, we were extra careful and I was referred to a specialist. I hate injections and I was horrified when I was told I had to have one in my stomach every day to stop blood clots. My husband, who has always been supporting and caring, volunteered to do it for me. It was impossible for me to even look at the needle. It was real torture, but I was ready to do whatever it took to save our third baby.

Everything worked out, and we were extremely excited to find out that we were going to have a baby boy. We named him Harry. He was growing well until a few tests indicated there were complications. This led us to make very difficult decisions. We lost Harry at 21 weeks in March 2021.

This time, it was different. I could not handle my emotional pain. I felt paralysed.

Life is mysterious like that. Sometimes it will throw great things at you and sometimes it tests you by making you go through very difficult situations. No matter how good, strong, or happy you may be, everyone inevitably encounters challenges. When things get tough, we have only two choices. We can let the situation or our emotions get to us, making us feel broken, or we can uplift ourselves and transform whatever pain we have into possibilities and power.

Building resilience is the ultimate key to turning any challenge into growth. Everyone has the power to develop a positive, uplifting and resilient mindset. In my experience, the road to success was paved with a lot of challenges. But you will never experience resilience unless you are faced with challenges. And failing in what you had planned to achieve is just a stepping stone that everyone goes through to grow. You are stronger than you think.

Any problematic situation can bend you, but you have the power not to let it break you. No matter how many times you fall, simply get back up and keep on moving forward. The next time you look back, you will be amazed at how much growth you acquired.

In The Middle Of Difficulty Lies Opportunity
I met Chloë Bisson in some of Jessen's training and I really wanted to work with her. My dream came true when the

Queens In Business Club was founded. I was so excited when we were informed that there were four more Co Founders - Carrie, Shim, Sunna and Tanya - and that I would be able to be coached by them all. The majority of my growth has come from having the right guidance, motivation and inspiration from mentors and the right network.

Around the same time, I was invited to enter a speaking competition which led me to share my story openly. And only a couple of months later, wrote my first book, Left In Peace, Not Pieces which became a number one international best seller in five countries and seven categories on Amazon. Not long after that, I also spoke on stage as a panelist at the Queens In Business event, Reign Like A Queen.

You see, opportunities won't find you if you are nowhere to be found. Before you find it, you must be looking for it!

The question is how do you identify opportunities and what can you do to make sure you do not miss out on things that could help you or your business grow?

1. Identify your values. Who are you and what is it that you do? What do you believe in and what is your purpose?

2. Say yes and figure it out. When you say yes, you are empowering yourself to believe in your skills and abilities. You will never grow in your career unless you seek new opportunities. Some opportunities may never strike again.

3. Make learning a habit. There is nothing worse than relying on luck rather than facts. If you are in business, you must know your target audience and what they currently invest in so that you can find opportunities to tap into this.

4. Perceive yourself as an expert. If you want to be influential, do things that empower you so that you feel confident to show up and share your wisdom with the world. Remember, you do not have to be perfect. Perfectionism is the enemy of actions.

5. Be smart. Put yourself in a position that makes it easier for opportunities to come to you. Update your social media information so that when people find you, it is clear what you do and what you can bring to the table. The way you position yourself will differ from others because what will work for one may not work for another.

Managing Energy And Mindset

Sometimes life gets increasingly demanding and we tend to multitask and wear many different hats. Whether it is in our personal, professional, or business life, most of us thrive on accomplishing a lot in very little time. Working hard is perceived differently by different people, but when we're doing what we love, we tend to push ourselves to our limits.

This often leaves us feeling overwhelmed.

My personal life circumstances made my body feel fragile and my energy level became really low. I was not as strong as I used to be.

From being a very active person, I suddenly could not do anything. My goals were clear, however, I felt paralysed, and I could not take any action. I was finding it challenging to make even simple decisions. The only way I managed to stay on top of everything was by learning how to navigate through tough times.

Despite how I felt, I knew I could not carry on feeling and living this way. I needed good habits that could help me get back on track. When you're struggling, it is super important to set clear food and exercise habits. These vital habits will determine your energy levels and inevitably impact the actions you take in seeking growth.

For example, instead of saying that you want to start eating healthy, it is best to have an eating plan. That way, you will spend less time making decisions which will leave you less stressed and more organised and motivated.

Successful people have great habits. With the same inspiration and much effort, I started planning my day and pushed myself to commit to some good habits. Apart from my normal routine, there are four habits that I personally developed and follow religiously.

1. Learn something new every day. I am constantly learning new things that can support me in my business. For example, I learned how to use Canva, Active Campaign and how to make professional videos.

2. Get Inspired. I listen to my mentor daily to stay motivated. I also listen to podcasts, watch motivational speeches on YouTube and read positive stories.

3. Self-reflect. I take time for myself to reflect on where I am now, what I have achieved and what I need to do. I gain clarity when I spend some quiet time alone, sometimes early in the morning or at night.

4. Exercise daily. I have made it a habit to exercise at least 15 minutes daily. This boosts my energy level and makes me feel more confident.

These simple and realistic habits became embedded with my other routines, and I no longer have to think about them. This frees space in my mind to work on bigger decisions and goals.

The process of launching my business was not easy, but I learned the importance of planning to increase productivity. This, in turn, improves work-life balance, keeping you in a positive and uplifted mindset, and allows more room for new challenges and opportunities.

The three strategies I used to work smart are:

1. Delegate. This is an essential skill to master. Instead of trying to accomplish everything, focus on tasks that will have the greatest long-term result.

2. Chunk tasks. For example, if you receive emails all day long, instead of being reactive and answering them all day, be more proactive and schedule blocks during the day to check and respond to them. The key here is that timing is everything. There is a certain time of the day when certain types of tasks impact your productivity. When chunking tasks and deciding when to complete them, take into consideration your concentration and energy levels.

3. Less is more. Having a long to-do list can make you feel like you are setting yourself up for failure and will make you unproductive. A smaller, more realistic to-do list is more achievable and less intimidating.

Starting up and running a business can be lonely. Most people believe that they can achieve their goals alone and that's okay. However, life can be hard and there are always obstacles on our path to growth. During these periods, there is nothing better than having the right people around you, perhaps friends or mentors who are ready to listen, advise you and support you to propel forward.

If you want to grow and make positive changes in your life, the people around you will have a critical impact on your energy and probability for growth. The right circle of influence will raise the bar and can help you get out of your comfort zone. I was fortunate to have approached the right people to support me through my challenges.

It is also important to remove Negative Nellys from your life. Negative people can hold you back and discourage you from achieving your limitless potential. Removing them from the equation will give you more energy to take progressive steps that will allow you to become more positive, successful, and fulfilled.

Positive people always bring out the best in you, will be there to support you through challenges, help you achieve your goals and will be there to celebrate your success.

List down five names of the people you want to keep in your close circle - both professional and personal.

If you do not like where you are right now, seek change. Challenges will always occur so brace yourself and trust that this is a crucial part of your journey. After all, this is what makes life interesting and overcoming obstacles is what makes life meaningful. Stay committed and make space for adjustments along the way. Remember, the person who is most flexible wins. The key is to keep on moving forward.

About Me

I am an inspirational business lecturer, international number one best-selling author, business start-up award winner, international public speaker, Founder of the Uplift Academy, proud wife and mother to my daughter and African grey parrot.

I have had the privilege of training thousands of people in business and believe that life should not be a struggle. That's why I help working adults become their own bosses. I have a passion for sharing my knowledge and empowering people to achieve greater success by working on their terms.

Ever since I was a little girl, education was my priority, so much so that the last dissertation I handed in was on my daughter's due date. Education has been my life, which led me to become an educator and lecturer for fifteen years. I worked very hard and always reinvested all the money I earned into my learning, acquiring way too many diplomas, an undergraduate, two postgraduates and a Master's degree.

I always felt fortunate that I never had any gap in employment and had been headhunted four times.

But life and my mindset changed after becoming a mum. I understood how much strength women have and how we endure much emotional and physical pain but can bounce back and smile. The world is full of talent, yet people live their lives through limited beliefs. I want to help people unleash their inner powers so that they do not have to go through the struggles that we assume is normal.

This chapter is dedicated to all women in the world. To my mum, the most muscular woman I know. To my husband Peter, who has been my most incredible support. To my family and friends for their love. To my amazing in-laws. To Jessen, Chloë, Carrie, Shim, Sunna and Tanya for their guidance and inspiration.

Burn, Baby, Burn

Cristina Cozzone
Founder of ME Mastery and
Strategic Intervention Life Coach
#1 Best-Selling and Multi Award-Winning
International Author

"There is a light within each of us that can never be diminished or extinguished. It can only be obscured by forgetting who we are" -- Deepak Chopra

I believe that we all have a light inside us. It doesn't matter whom or what we believe in. It is a part of us and it doesn't mind what we call it. We are born to radiate this light out into the world.

I am in the business of sparking the light. I have been in this business since I was a little girl, though I didn't realise I could create a career out of it until I was 33 years old. Little did I know, I had already brought it to every interaction, personally and professionally.

I was born to the most wonderful, big, LOUD, loving Italian family. I was praised and celebrated for being uniquely me without question. I felt their love unconditionally.

I was short and skinny and raised to believe I was big and strong - I could do anything! When I was quiet and shy, I felt safe. When I was ready to perform my musical and dancing talents, I was given a stage. I was naturally both, depending on whether I trusted those around me at the time.

Once, on a family road trip, our RV got a flat tire. Inside the shop, my three-year-old tiny self climbed to the top of a tire stack to sing, 'America the Beautiful' for the entire lobby. The song was in my favourite movie, Pollyanna, a Disney classic with Haley Mills. The movie is set in a grumpy, sleepy town when a curious and somewhat mischievous outsider - in the best way - creates a stir that begins to spark gladness wherever she goes. By the end of the film she has the whole town looking for the bright side of life.

I share this story because it explains a bit about who I am. Just like Pollyanna, I like to bring gladness wherever I go and I do my best to look for the good even when it is difficult to find. To this day, my older sister will chuckle and call me out when I am being a "Pollyanna".

The World May Try To Dim Your Light

When I got into the school system, my perception of myself started to shift. I realised that love, acceptance, and understanding were not unconditional in this setting - they had to be earned. What was more confusing, was that the rules on how to earn it seemed to change by the day. Though I do believe in earning someone's trust, I also believe that all humans deserve a basic understanding, acceptance and kindness.

I did have great teachers but sadly for me, it only took one to dim my light and shake my confidence. My kindergarten teacher, who on the outside seemed really nice, would pass out stickers at the end of the day IF we were good. Since it is in my nature to be a "good girl" this system worked out pretty well for me. Then one day, it changed.

We were filling in a worksheet and I got stuck on the word "bag". I knew that I needed the "b" sounding letter, I just couldn't remember what direction to write it towards. I was getting nervous since most of my class had gotten up to play already.

I looked at the alphabet board at the top of the class hoping to find a clue that would jog my brain but it wasn't working. As each student left the table I got more and more anxious and confused. There were only a few of us left and one girl happened to be right next to me. I wanted to see how far she was because at this point I was more concerned with being left alone at the table than writing the correct letter, when I felt my teacher standing over me and with a harsh tone that thundered through the room, she called me a "cheater". I can still feel the stares of my classmates and desire to shrink away.

I'm not sure I fully understood what cheating was or even if I knew I wasn't supposed to look at another person's paper. The "good girl" in me was wounded. I was not the type to do anything against the rules.

As a former teacher, I can see the mistakes that happened here. This was our first introduction to letters and we weren't given any guidance or help. Our teacher wasn't even sitting at the table with us. Not to mention that it is very common for all young students to mix the lowercase letters b, d, g, q and p.

However, I wasn't a teacher, I was a five-year-old. I learned something that day and the years afterwards - I was different and therefore not enough. I later found out that she met with my parents to tell them to give up hope because I would never be smart enough to get into college (at age 5?!). I didn't need to know that she had labelled me stupid, I could feel it. There was nothing I could do right in her eyes no matter how hard I tried.

My parents, the amazing people they are, disagreed and started advocating for my education and future. In the third grade I was tested and to my surprise, in contrary to my teacher's belief, I have an exceptionally high IQ! I also had dyslexia and ADHD which was calmed down with fantastic tutors that taught me how my brain works, and teachers that were open to educating more than one learning type.

Still, the damage of being categorised as stupid and less than my fellow classmates for three years had already been done. Even after years of excellent grades and achievements, after getting into college and graduating with honours, the thought lingered in the back of my mind, "It's not enough, I am not enough."

Every time I was up against an obstacle I fought and conquered it, however I still struggled against that ingrained bullsh*t belief. Thank goodness for the light that burns regardless. That light kept me pushing past what others expected, it kept me pushing past my own comfort zone, and my own limiting beliefs.

This one bad teacher from my childhood unknowingly stayed with me for most of my life. I learned from that teacher that I was stupid and that being unique was bad. As most do, I learned to protect myself. I created a person that had to be absolutely perfect, work harder than anyone else, stay quiet, keep her head down and people please like no other. I would no longer bring attention to myself and that girl that loved the spotlight hid in the background in fear of failure and being judged. It was exhausting to play a role that was not natural to my identity.

That teacher thought she could declare my whole life by her very small interaction with me in KINDERGARTEN! She lost that bet and this is what I learned, we are going to come up against these types of people in life. Particularly in business, we are going to hear the word 'NO' a lot! Your friends and family may be those people. They may think you're insane for starting your own business!

This is when you remember that no else but you can declare your future. YOU are the director of your life! No teacher, family member, spouse, friend, or former boss can claim your future.

A Flickering Flame

At nine years old, I was diagnosed with leukemia. From this point forward, cancer became my biggest and best life teacher. I realised then that if I could get through that, I really could do anything! I was now a walking testament that even in the darkness moments, we can still find the light.

Growing up I knew I wanted to help others. My cancer helped me see the power and strength of a child and how often it is not recognised by adults. My parents were amazing and understood that I was going through an adult trauma and decided to respect me like an adult. They were honest with me and never hid the hard things so I knew I could trust everything they said - good or bad. They did so with grace and I felt seen.

When I got back to the "real world", many adults would baby me and talk around me like many adults do unknowingly to children. It made me mad - I had literally pulled myself from the grips of death and *I'm* the less wise one of the two of us? I vowed to always remember that feeling and to never, ever treat a child as if they were less-than because they had less time on Earth.

When you know the truth, it doesn't mean that everything else magically gets easier. I knew this rationally but not always emotionally. Like a flickering flame, I would still waver between being brave and being scared.

Nonetheless, it taught me to follow my dreams and to make today count because each day is a blessing. It is one of the reasons I believe I made such an outstanding teacher, because I saw each new day as a new start. The challenges I faced gave me determination, resiliency, and constant never-ending improvement. Without them, I would not be the person I am today.

Ignite The Light Within

My passion for service found its way into teaching. Surprise! I became a pre-k teacher. I wanted to build children up for the world they were likely to experience. I wanted to be sure they knew their value and worth so if anyone came into their life that made them feel less-than, they would know the truth and have an invisible protective shield around them.

This is so much a part of my true mission that I am in tears just writing it. To think that any child would not be loved just for being their beautiful unique self still breaks my heart. So that is what I taught. I taught kindness, self-love, celebration of differences and taught my students to speak up for themselves. This to me was so much more important than letters and numbers - though we did learn that too!

My mission was to be the teacher each child needed, not the teacher I thought I should be or what administration wanted me to be but what they needed individually. The world has grown with us and it is common for businesses to recognise that there are different types of learners and different personality types but in the education system it is still very much a square peg, round hole situation - despite some teachers' attempts for change.

I LOVED teaching. I can't even explain the joy I had watching my students light up every time their little brains put something new together. Reaching 20 students a year was powerful and rewarding but if I wanted to make a bigger impact on the world I was going to have to be brave and open myself up to something more.

This Girl Is On Fire

"Mom, you have to watch this with me!" I was watching Oprah when a gigantic man popped on the screen and I was completely mesmerised by his message. That man was Tony Robbins and he was taking Oprah through his Unleash The Power Within event.

During this event, Tony has participants WALK ON FIRE so that they can see that anything is possible with the right focus. As Tony was getting Oprah "into state", I was standing, following every direction as if the fire was in front me. I got myself into state and in my mind I walked over those hot coals. I told my mom with bright eyes and certainty in my voice, "Someday, I am going to do that!" It is funny how we can say things with such conviction and never know how it will come to be. About five years later in 2018, I became a fire walker and in 2021 I went back to do it again!

Mindset. It is all about mindset and what we focus on. To walk on fire and not get burned you have to be in control of your thoughts. If you think you will burn, you will burn and it hurts! I know because the first time I walked on fire I had to learn a valuable lesson. Not to get too deep into this story, but because I couldn't feel the coals (I was doing so well) I second guessed it and thought for sure it had to be fake. My focus quickly shifted and I felt the heat of the coals and burnt the bottom of my right foot enough to know it was real.

The second time, I knew it was all mindset! I knew that I would walk across those coals without a burn. I visualised that outcome over and over. I replayed it in my head, said all the empowering words, got up to the fire and felt the fear rise. Listen, just because I was better prepared didn't make it any less scary! But it did help me quiet the fear and make positivity the bigger voice in my head. That night I walked on fire and felt nothing, not a single burn!

This is a beautiful lesson for business. We will come up against moments that are scary, but the more we practise, the better we will get. You have to keep pushing yourself past the fear.

Going to seminar after seminar I began to notice how many of us adults were there trying to let go of the limiting beliefs we had created in childhood - and ones they gathered while in the school system particularly. I was shocked to find so many people felt the same way I did - that they weren't cared for in the way they needed to be.

146

Because of my unique path, I had learned to create my own little university. I would write up what I wanted to learn, then I would create a syllabus with a list of books and action steps to create my personal growth.

I created a school for myself for learning the things I felt like I should have been taught as a kid, and this eventually became ME Mastery. Did you know, adults' eyes light up the exact same way a child's does when they have made a realisation? This is the best part of my mission - getting to witness the light in another spark and shine again.

Let Your Light Shine!

Though I am writing this to hopefully inspire you to see that change is possible for everyone including you, I am also writing this as a reminder to myself. See, I tend to forget all that I have already accomplished. You may be the same. My guess is that if you are reading this book you are also an achiever.

Achievers are my favourite type of people, but we do have our faults. One being that once we have achieved something, we are straight onto the next thing with very little celebration. It has been one of my biggest lessons in life to learn to stop and celebrate each win - big or small - before moving forward.

When I am looking at a big year of things I have set out to accomplish and I'm not in the right mindset a few things may happen:

1. I may beat myself up for not accomplishing these things sooner.
2. I may get super overwhelmed by my grand plans.
3. I may think to myself, "Who do you think you are for being so bold?" and question if I am worthy.

On the other hand, when I am in control of my mindset, all these excuses get immediately squashed.

Growth is like watching a child grow. They grow a little bit everyday but because we are watching their constant little transitions, we can't see the big change. Then a family member will come over and say, "Oh my goodness, she has gotten so big since the last time I saw her!" That is when we are prompted to really look and are surprised at how much they have grown.

Remember, big growth doesn't happen overnight, despite what social media wants us to believe. Even the most successful entrepreneurs, those now billionaires, will say something along the lines of, "I was an overnight success... 16 years in the making."

Growth is something you are doing a little bit of every day. You may not see it, but with each new client, course and networking event, you are building the blocks to your desired outcome.

When we take moments to reflect we create time to collect evidence of our growth. This is like seeing the first day of school pictures vs the last day. When you are feeling overwhelmed and stuck, look back at your evidence file to see how far you have truly come. You may surprise yourself that you are a lot closer to your goals than you recognised - celebrate that!

Growth is momentum. With growth comes believing in yourself, and in believing in yourself, you create more growth.

See? Growth happens whether you pay attention to it or not. If you are going to grow, you may as well point yourself in the right direction. So, get clear on what your goals are, place them on your bathroom mirror so that you can see them every time you brush your teeth. Our brains are really good at taking care of the rest. Of course, you do have to take action, but just seeing your goals in front of you will create an unconscious desire to take steps towards that direction.

Growth is community, collaboration and mirroring those who have gone before you because success leaves clues.

I believe in you and your dreams. You can create the change you want in your life and if you want to supercharge that change and shorten the time, consider working with a coach, mentor and/or become part of a community to keep you accountable in taking action to be the fire that you want to see in the world.

Lightning Sparks A Wildfire

I believe we all have a light inside us. That light can dim and grow many times over a lifetime or just in a day. What I have come to believe through my experience of being a teacher and coach is that most of us have gotten comfortable with our light dimmed down. We can still see just fine so we forget to notice that we used to illuminate much brighter.

Have you witnessed a moment when a spark of light shines in another? That spark, that flash of light, that is the currency of my passion. It has been the one thing I have been drawn to my entire life, helping others create it themselves and holding onto it for myself.

I like to think I walk around with this spark most days, but then there are the days I just feel grey. Have you been there? What about the days waaaay past grey - when your light is on its way to being extinguished?

I work with a lot of women and I have seen how we tend to allow our light to dim for the betterment of others. Why? Because naturally, women who live in their feminine, tend to be nurturers - givers. Women will give all day to their partners, their children, their jobs and feel selfish when taking time for themselves.

In my conversations with these women, I have come up with a quote that maybe I created or heard somewhere else but it works, "You have to be selfish to give selflessly". In terms of business, how can you serve your clients, if you can't serve yourself? If your light is burnt out, who will take over in carrying out your mission? Remember, I am a huge advocate for children, so if you happen to be a mama, I am telling you, you must care for yourself first - yes, even before your children!

Let's take a deep breath. I would like you to remember a time when you felt completely "on fire", full of vibrant, radiant energy. What were you doing? What did it feel like in your body? How were you breathing? Where was your focus and what types of things were you saying to yourself in that moment?

Take a moment to think about it then write it down.

Did you do it!? Congratulations! You just wrote down your unique recipe for feeling "on fire"!

Spread that fire like wildfire! If you need help sparking it or simply brightening it up, find someone you can trust to elevate you to the next level. There is always another level and you don't have to do it alone!

I will be honest, I am not under the illusion that I have all the answers. In fact, I never have the answers for my clients because they already have the answers for themselves - I just help them find them.

I am in the business of sparking the light and feeding the fire. The most rewarding part of my mission is seeing the light rise in someone. That moment when they come to realisation, an aha moment, and when they recognise that it was always there inside themselves waiting to be reignited.

When you walk this world, radiating your light, it sparks the light in others and you create that wildfire. When you show up uniquely you, you give permission for others to shine their unique gifts. You become the spark. You were always the spark. So, burn, baby, burn!!!

About Me

I am the Founder of ME Mastery and a strategic intervention coach. I am in the business of sparking the light in others. I believe we all have a light inside us and when we shine our light brightly we make a positive impact on the world that spreads like wildfire.

I am a number one best-selling author for my international book, When the Universe Whispered Hush, which has helped children all over the world to remember to look for the good even when it may seem impossible!

I was born and raised in Northbrook, Illinois, USA, where I currently live with my husband. At nine years old, I was diagnosed with leukemia (ALL) and needed a bone marrow transplant. I felt it was important for kids, similar to myself, to have a book that explained what it was like to have childhood cancer.

As a result, I am also recognised for my book, Me and My Marrow, published in multiple languages including Spanish and Japanese. The book received the Health Information Award for Best Patient Education Book and the American Medical Writers Award for Patient Information in 2000.

I have been featured on the cover of the Chicago Tribune and on WGN News. I have also had the pleasure of being featured on multiple YouTube channels.

Building community is extremely important to me and I am tremendously proud to be a Founding Member of the Queens In Business Club and the American representative in this book!

I dedicate this chapter to my adoring husband for being my partner in this life journey and to my "big Italian family" who have always been in my corner cheering me on!

There Can Be Miracles When You Believe!

Caroline Martin
NLP Trainer and Leadership Coach
Enabling Wings

"We need to reshape our own perception of how we view ourselves. We have to step up as women and take the lead"
-- Beyoncé Knowles

There once was an intelligent academic young lady. She lived in a small commuter town in the heart of the English Essex countryside. Her parents moved away from city life when she was just a baby.

The young lady worked hard at school, she would engage in chatter with her friends, and most of the time she was a model pupil. She helped at lunch time, she was interested and studious in class, and she achieved excellent grades.

While she had many friends at school, relationships with her peers were often a challenge, as it is for many young girls. I'm sure you can relate... girls can be lovely one minute and the next... well... they can be quite the opposite!

The young lady had a handful of close friends and one best friend. Collectively they were a competitive bunch who would compete to read books and achieve the next level of academic study. At the age of 11, the young lady and her best friend embraced their creativity and became the entrepreneurs of the playground. In the winter of 1988, they commandeered one of the school mum's knitting machines. They worked hard every day after school, making royal blue scarves and the newly fashionable snoods to match their school uniforms and they sold them to their peers on their lunch break.

Come Easter, the girls dug out a plaster of Paris mould set, bought cooking chocolate and set to work making chocolate animals in their parents' kitchen. They shared the delights at school… health and safety wasn't really considered back then. In the summer term FIMO became a craze - you know, that coloured clay stuff that turns hard when you bake it in the oven? The girls set to work making animal themed earrings and models. They were in their element and the playground was buzzing with customers queuing for their wares on a daily basis.

The young lady started secondary school where children from several local schools combined to join the high school. She and her best friend had chosen to be together and were in the same class. They were thrust into a new world with less play and more study, and the fun stuff started to dwindle.

A short way into the first school year, the young lady became ill and was taken to hospital with a tummy complaint. She was away from school for a few weeks and in that time, she didn't hear from her friend. How would she? There were no mobiles at that time, no internet, no WhatsApp. At the young age of 12, children hadn't even started using landlines… those old phones that were attached to the wall with a cord, do you remember those?

The young lady returned to school after several weeks of bed rest, unsure of what to expect because she had been disconnected from her world. To her surprise, her friend wasn't there. Silently, she got on with her work and connected with the other girls at break times. She wondered where her friend was, was she ill too?

After many days, possibly weeks, she asked her form tutor, "Miss... Where's Georgina?" The teacher seemed to ignore her.

The next day she asked again, "Miss... Where's Georgina?" The teacher seemed busy, and she wasn't sure if she had been heard or not but something inside her told her not to persist.

A few more days passed. The young lady, knowing that she had been very ill in hospital, was getting rather worried about her friend and so she asked again, "Miss... Where's Georgina?"

The teacher put down her pen, slammed her fist on the desk, and pushed herself up to a standing position. Leaning forward with both hands on the desk, she looked the young lady directly in the eyes. "For goodness sake child! Georgina has moved to another class!"

The young lady's heart stopped. There was silence, she felt confused, this didn't make sense and so she asked, "Err why?"

The teacher stared at her in anger and after a pause, she said, "Because YOU... are a HORRIBLE CHILD!"

The young lady was taken aback. She felt physically winded by the words. She bowed her head and left the classroom, upset, gutted, frightened by what the teacher had said. No cross words had passed between her and Georgina, what on earth had she done?

False Evidence Appearing Real (FEAR)

The weeks, months and years passed. The young lady occasionally saw Georgina with a group of girls at school, some of whom had been their old friends at primary school. If eye contact was made, both girls would sheepishly look away. No words were shared, no conversations were had, no questions were asked.

The young lady made some wonderful new friends and for the most part she enjoyed school life but she doubted herself a lot. That teacher's words often echoed in her head.

"You... are a HORRIBLE CHILD!"

Those words stopped her from trying, those words made her overthink every conversation, those words held her back.

The young lady continued through high school and got great grades. She excelled in her work experience and secured a holiday job at a local insurance company which then led to a full-time position.

The young lady thrived in her career
The 'little star' secured promotions year after year!
She was a staunch pessimist despite her success,
never good enough in her own head.
She didn't believe the compliments she received.
Always the 'horrible child' she perceived.

Fast forward to 2012, she had two school-aged children and was working part-time and she had a yearning to get back on the career ladder. One day, her sister arrived at her house with a bag of skincare. She had joined a network marketing company and was absolutely pumped with excitement. Curious, the young lady joined too, she had lost her way a little when becoming a mum and she wanted to progress with something that she could do around the children. The lady (not so young by this time) attended the training and was fascinated by the swift success of some of the people in this business. She asked what they were doing, what was it that was creating such positive change? She was told, "We read."

"Oh, I read too," she responded with a smile. "I don't get a lot of time because I have two children but I often enjoy a chick lit book on holiday."

"Not that sort of book. We read self-help books."

The lady felt her eyes roll and she politely said, "Oh, okay." She didn't verbalise her thoughts but inside she was thinking, "No offence but I'm an insurance professional." She was damned if she was going to spend her evenings reading self-help books like Bridget Jones, all by herself, crying into a wine bottle (even though the latter had been known from time to time).

The ladies insisted that this was the 'training' she needed but there was no way she was doing that!

As the months passed, she watched from the side-lines as more people took the stage with their success stories. Perhaps there was something in these books? Perhaps she should try?

The lady started to read and she discovered that most of these books were written by highly successful people, sharing their stories and strategies of success. These people thought the way she did, these people overcame the negative thoughts in their heads. She began to realise that there were specific things that she could do to transform her life. She let her curiosity lead her and in the process, she became braver, more confident, and started to learn to step out of her comfort zone. These books were expanding her thinking and opening her mind to a whole new world of opportunity.

A couple of years later, social media started to boom and the lady came across her primary school best friend. Georgie appeared in the 'people you may know' list, but while she had a hidden curiosity, she was too scared to reopen that wound and she repeatedly avoided the temptation.

One day, after several glasses of wine she was scrolling and then… oops… friend request sent. Oh gosh. Should she undo this? What on earth had she done?

Moments later a message popped up: Georgina has accepted your friend request.

Oh no. What now?

The ladies bravely typed small talk for several hours, neither broaching the subject of year 7 at secondary school. Georgie had also worked in the finance industry for many years. She took redundancy to pursue her entrepreneurial side. She was now the local Willy Wonka with a thriving online sweet business.

The two stayed in touch and Georgie became the lady's best customer in her new network marketing business.

A year or so later, the lady had a message out of the blue. Georgie was having a house gathering with some of the girls from their primary school class. Should she go? Remembering both happy and challenging times as a little girl, she wasn't sure. Thoughts swirled round and round in her head before she took the step to accept.

Armed with a cheeky bottle of red wine for courage, a bouquet of flowers and a list of quick get-away excuses, she gingerly knocked on the door. She was greeted warmly with familiar faces from years gone by.

The wine flowed and Georgie asked what happened to the young lady at school and the young lady asked why she left the class. Holding her breath waiting for the reply. Georgie said, "I didn't like the teacher, she was horrible to me when you weren't there and I was moved. Where did you go?"

The lady was speechless. Almost 25 years had passed! Tears welling in her eyes, she swigged her glass of wine and said, "You mean it wasn't my fault?"

"Your fault? Why would it have been your fault, you weren't there!"

The lady, shocked, told her what the teacher had said and replied, "But you ignored me in the playground!"

"I thought you were ignoring me! I didn't know what to say!"

Both ladies stood for a moment, stunned, silently reflecting on the loss. They had both been running with their own assumptions in their heads, creating deep limiting beliefs. Suddenly the years began to melt away...

That lady was me.

Reframe Your Thoughts For A Better Outcome

Fast forward again and my business led me to someone else I went to school with. This guy kept telling me that I would be a great coach. There was that eye rolling again. I went to the gym but I couldn't be a personal trainer. I had no idea what coaching was or why he was saying this to me. Again, I politely nodded while thinking he was a little crazy. But he saw something in me that I couldn't see for myself yet.

After the separation from my kids' dad, on the first weekend away from my children in January 2016, a free coaching course appeared on Facebook. My children had been my whole purpose for over a decade and I didn't quite know how I would cope without them. I thought about what my friend had said, and knowing that I would be alone, I decided that this would fill my time.

It was a big step for me, a step beyond reading books and attending seminars with people I knew. I had no idea what it was or where it would lead me.

At the event, I realised that the concept of coaching was not new to me. For example, I had used goal setting regularly in my corporate life. I joined a professional coaching course in April and then began my NLP journey in October. I was building a toolkit of practical processes that worked to help others step out of their comfort zones and move towards achieving their goals. This time though, these goals were not set by a manager. This was for me, helping me achieve personal success.

Once again, I was lit up seeing the incredible change in others. Only this time it wasn't the books. With these new skills, I became a catalyst for lasting change. I became even more addicted to exploring how the human mind works and realised that the age old saying was wrong. You *can* teach an old dog new tricks! I was becoming living proof that you can change your thinking and when you do, it absolutely changes your life and I have been blessed with helping others to do the same!

We all go through a rollercoaster of experiences on our journey through life. Sometimes we are riding the highs and sometimes we are in the terrifying depths of the lows. In that darkness, it can feel like there is a wall preventing us from moving forward. Each phase of our life teaches us something. As we learn and grow, we won't always make perfect choices but progress leads to happiness.

Have you ever learned more information about a situation and that situation suddenly seems different in your mind?

It was easy to blame the teacher for how Georgie and I both felt - what an awful thing she had said to me. Who behaves like that, especially someone that I should have been able to trust?

The reality is that we did have a choice. I often wonder how our lives would have been different if only Georgie and I had chosen to speak. I chose to believe the teacher and to let that negative voice control my actions. What would have happened had I chosen to behave differently?

With my new reframed way of thinking about that particular teacher, I now realise that teacher was probably angry and upset at what had happened. Who knows what was going on in her life at the time? Had she received negative feedback about the situation? Perhaps she hadn't quite managed to process it yet. Perhaps she was just having a bad day? Then up pops me, a bit naggy and I just happened to press the hot buttons! I'm sure that all of us, at some point in our lives, have said something to someone that we don't really mean in a moment of despair, perhaps without even considering the consequences.

Before I really delved into personal development, I was a negative Nelly. That's quite a natural place to be as our brains are hardwired to look for danger to protect us. My life was a reflection of the programmes that I consumed on a daily basis. I was fearful and blamed others for how my life was turning out and I had stopped taking action to improve myself. I believed that life was hard, I gave up on the dreams I had as a little girl. Those dreams were never possible for someone like me, I wasn't deserving. The list went on and on! The negative things I thought about myself literally took over my brain and stopped me from attending social events and even a friend's wedding!

My journey is teaching me that everything happens for a reason and that the darkest times often teach us something that we will need later on in life. I now know that the way that I think can change and by making those changes, I can open my eyes to new beliefs.

Now, I help others change the limiting stories that they tell themselves. Changing patterns of behaviour requires work and you must keep your mind in check!

My gift to you here, is to invite you to start challenging your thinking. Grab yourself a piece of paper and a pen and reflect:

- What are the stories from your past that are holding you back?
- What are the limiting beliefs that you are telling yourself in those stories? (I'm not good enough, I can't)
- Change the statements to positive beliefs (I am good enough, I can.)
- What evidence do you have that those positive statements are true?

For example:

Perhaps you have a story about something that you did in your past and you have started telling yourself, "I am a bad friend". Every time a challenge crops up, your brain will look for things to validate that belief until you change it. Change the belief to a positive one for example: "I am a good friend", and then write a list of evidence to back up the new belief.

Give yourself permission to think about things differently and let go of the trap that these beliefs may have over you. Allow yourself to learn that there is another way and that all those dreams which you had as a child can still be achievable, no matter what your age or experience is. I promise you that if you change the way you look at things, the things you look at will change.

Sadly, Georgie tragically passed away in 2017. I miss her terribly. I am so very grateful that she re-entered my life to reminisce and for the additional precious memories we shared. She helped me understand that I wasn't a horrible child after all. She reconnected me with the playful entrepreneurial spirit we had as young girls. You may think I'm bonkers but I know she is cheering me on with each success and nudging me forward when things get too tough and I feel like giving up.

I am now very fortunate that my continued extensive study has gifted me the skills to become a Leadership Coach and NLP Trainer. I'm sure I won't stop there with my learning and desire to help leaders become their best selves and to help their teams.

If you are reading this and saying to yourself, "I am not a leader", then stop right there! You are showing up here for yourself, perhaps for inspiration, perhaps because you, like me, are looking for better ways. These are fundamental leadership qualities and whether you work for yourself or are employed by another, you are a leader!

About Me

I am a dedicated mum of two teens, certified NLP Trainer, accredited coach, five-time fire walker, aspiring nutritionist and Founder of my coaching business, Enabling Wings.

I have experienced incredible transformation in my life, taking me from 'glass half empty Martin' - a cynical and protective person who is scared of change, to 'Caroline, positive and passionate'. It has taken years to connect my past and my learnings through life with my strengths, skills and opportunities, which now enable me to spread my own wings and be connected to my passions and live life with conscious purpose.

I have dedicated over 25 years to customer-oriented roles within the global commercial insurance sector. My focus was to facilitate excellence for bespoke customers and it gave me great pride to be able to positively impact so many customer journeys.

In 2012, I discovered personal development and started studying success and the power of the mind. I have invested in myself and followed my passion for life coaching, being trained by many experts including Tony Robbins, Dr Roe, Joe Vitale, Allan Kleynhans, NLP master trainers, Lisa De Rijk and John Thompson, NLP trainer Douglas De Souza and of course my NLP mentor and master trainer, Steve Payne.

I am truly grateful to my family, friends, peers, teachers and clients for helping me on my journey - I am learning from all of you. I have a special place in my heart for my co-pilot, Dean Swift, who is always cheering me on from the side-lines and giving me a positive nudge, without whom I wouldn't have achieved many of my goals.

Over the last few years, I have seen a real increase in the momentum for corporate appreciation of personal development, recognising the link between personal wellbeing, employee engagement and indeed corporate productivity. Corporations do have the power to enable many individuals to achieve great successes, and so, I now dedicate my time to coaching individuals and businesses to create alignment, and to helping others to overcome challenges.

This chapter of the book is dedicated to my dear departed friend, Georgie Moon.

Under Construction

Christina Robinson
Managing Director
Green Umbrella Marketing Ltd

"The first step to getting somewhere is to decide you're not going to stay where you are" -- J P Morgan

There are so many places to begin this story. A raft of challenges that anyone reading this could relate to; physical pain, emotional pain, financial pain, spiritual pain - I have stories for them all.

So, envision this, you go to sleep in a world where pain is your companion, survival is your norm and you have fully surrendered to the fact that the best you can hope for is less than average. You're at terms with your 'lot' in life and as you drift into that sleep, the thought lingers that if the worst thing that could happen right now is to never wake again, you're OK with that. In fact, it would be a relief.

In October 2016, I was finally on an operating table having the spinal surgery that had been considered 'urgent' for almost a year. Physical pain, especially at the level I was experiencing, can drag your mood down and affect your mental health. Now add to that the childhood trauma I was carrying, the abusive relationships of my past, the lasting effects of the depression I'd experienced in my twenties and again in my early thirties...

I was in pain.

Correction - pain was all I knew.

And yet, if you had known me back then, I would have told you I was at my peak! I had a job that I loved, in a business that I loved working for. An employer who I loved and colleagues who loved me. Although I had failed and was failing in every other area of my life, this - my job - THIS I was getting right.

If I take you back a year or two earlier, I was walking with my boss and Founder of Green Umbrella Marketing (GU). We were talking about her plans for the business and her plans for herself. She had sold a business prior to GU and we'd been talking about that experience when the conversation came around to what her exit strategy might be for this business. She said she never wanted to go through that experience again and that she would either look to create an MBO (Management Buy Out) or simply close things down over time.

I'm nodding along as she speaks because it all makes sense. It's completely logical and the kind of plan I would expect from the successful, inspiring female entrepreneur in front of me. And then she asks me, "Do you think you'd want to buy the business when the time comes?"

My inside voice is going, "You what mate? What just happened? Are you mad? That's never going to happen!"

My people-pleasing outside voice said, "Yes."

I had started working at Green Umbrella Marketing in January 2013 as a freelancer because I was a mature student at university who had dropped out.

With a young family, struggling to pay the bills and no skills outside of a previous career I didn't want to go back to, I had been thinking how I could start something myself and had considered starting a business managing social media for other people.

When looking into that, I discovered this little agency called Green Umbrella two minutes from my doorstep and had followed their Facebook page. The next weekend I saw an advert for a freelance position, applied, and within a week was part of team GU.

At that time, Green Umbrella ran a series of social media workshops and, due to my previous career in events, I became a part-time employee a few weeks later. My role within the business grew and grew, and fast forward six months, I had developed into the Founder's number two in the business.

But I had zero clue that I was seen in that way by her, or by anyone else in the business, or by our clients or partners. I was completely blind to it! Remember, my belief right now is that less than average is the best I can hope for. For years that is what I had been told by others as well as myself. It is what I believed.

No way could I buy a business! How would I even get the money together? I could barely afford a trip around the supermarket. If it wasn't for daily trips to the reduced counter at the local supermarkets my kids would be on a diet of Tesco Value fish fingers and not much else! Even if there was a way of getting the money together – I couldn't run a business! I didn't have the first clue!

I'd said "yes" because it was a throw away conversation and it was the right answer. You don't tell people their babies are ugly, and you don't tell your boss you'd never want to buy her business (aka her baby).

You Don't Always Have To Be Resilient

Back to 2016. I'm laid on an operating table counting backwards thinking, "I'll be unconscious in a minute but at last, whether I wake up again or not, I'll have some peace." Before I knew it, my eyes were opening and there was a weird sensation in my legs and feet. As my other senses started to kick in, I noticed a weird feeling.

It was a sheet laying on top of me.

For years, the physical pain had screamed above the numbness. I had accepted and lived daily with the pain for a long time - and I mean years before I asked for help or did anything to change the situation. In fact, I'd go and do things that I knew would aggravate my pain because I didn't want to miss out on things.

I had no idea just how limited I had become or how much I had been compensating just so I could continue to survive the other challenges I had been facing and also complete the most basic tasks. I was unaware, I was blind to it and so every day I was just reliving that same pain.

The next morning, I was encouraged to leave my hospital bed and stand. As I carefully swung my legs to the floor, I realised I didn't need to physically move them with my hands and as the sole of my foot connected with the floor I could feel the coldness of it. No pins and needles, no need to wait to squeeze and stretch my toes or stamp my feet to get the feeling they were there beneath me, ready to take my weight - none of that.

I could stand. And I could stand tall.

In that 24-hour period, it was like my body and my mind had reset. The weight of all the other pain I was carrying (the traumatic, spiritual, financial and emotional pain) did not come back to me until I was back at home still recovering from the operation.

A few days later, at home still recovering from surgery, an incident occurred that left me at my lowest point. The details of the incident are not relevant to this story, but what is relevant is that it left me thinking, "Why does this always happen to me?" A thought I'd had and an opinion I'd voiced many, many times over the years. I'd thought about it too many times in fact and never considered it beyond that.

We all experience challenges to varying degrees. Some people have experienced a catalogue of challenges. If, like me, you fall into the latter category you'll have perhaps shared the details with people who then say things like, "I don't know how you do it." In those situations I'd tend to deflect by saying something that brings the conversation to a close, hoping not to have to talk about too much more...

"God only sends us what we can cope with. How are YOU anyway?"

"Better me than someone else. Did you say you were going on holiday?"

"This too shall pass. How old is <insert child's name here> now?"

Whatever I would say it implied that I was OK with being the one who had these experiences. I was proud that I had the resilience to overcome what for some people would be their greatest fears or worst nightmares.

Spoiler alert: not only is it the opposite of OK that I have had the experiences I have had - it is the opposite of OK that I continued to invite chaos and trauma into my life by taking ownership of it like a badge of honour.

When The Only Option Is Change
Days after surgery, sitting on the edge of my bed with tears rolling in slow motion down my face, controlling my breath

so no one in the house could hear my distress, I had that familiar thought, "Why does this always happen to me?" Only this time, it was followed up with, "My life doesn't have to be this way."

In that moment I grew.

Everything I have achieved and will achieve stems back to that one moment, sat on my bed with tears streaming down my face. There was no 'why me?' moment followed by a pity party for one. It was a question - and it had to be answered.

I don't know why I have had the experiences I have but, in that moment, I knew that I needed to choose to have something different. It was the only thing in my control that could create long-term change.

For years, literally years, I had to look to make sure my feet were covered by the duvet at night, and every morning I had to wait to be able to stand because I didn't ask for help. I didn't make myself vulnerable and ask for help because I refused to admit the life I was living was wrong. I believed I was strong and that I had a high tolerance for pain. To become pain free, I had to become all the things I wasn't, take responsibility, ask for help, admit weakness and trust in a process.

What if I could apply that lesson elsewhere? What needs to happen to make my life better? Who do I need to be in order to achieve that?

Writing this now, I'm feeling that prickly sensation across my chest - a feeling of overwhelm and excitement. The cold fear of what I was about to do and the enormity of what I was about to embark upon. And at the same time, I know I've already done it and it's the reason I'm writing this!

I Deserve This

If I needed to take control of my life, I needed to take stock and truly reflect on where things were going wrong and in December 2016, I did just that. I created a vision of what my life should look like, what I deserved, and I made a plan.

- Cut toxic people out and spend more time with people who are positive
- Engage in self-development through reading one book a month
- Start journaling

Looking back, the changes I planned for that year were teeny tiny but they made all the difference! There were other things too, of course, but you get the gist.

In 2017, while my plan was being implemented, wow did my career jump forward! The Founder had begun to take time out of the business for her new developing passion. And as I grew and became more aware of my position and my abilities to run the business without her, she was able to increase that time out.

It was wonderful. I felt so empowered. I loved my job, I loved the responsibility and autonomy I had, I was being rewarded for it on a multitude of levels and I was fulfilled. People were calling me an expert and I was making a difference to them and their businesses. I was speaking at small events and travelling up and down the country meeting new people, closing business, building relationships. I was in my element.

Come spring 2018, things had reached a point where the Founder's new passion had developed into a hobby business. She was spending more and more time out and a meeting was called where a senior colleague and I asked her what her intentions were for the business.

Remember that question she'd asked me a few years prior? The one I'd said "yes" to thinking it was just a throw away conversation? Here I was, sitting as one of the three senior people in the business being asked again if I would want to buy the company.

Only this time, it was formal and not throwaway. This time there was the opportunity to do it as a partnership and now there was a time frame. If it was going to happen, the plan was it would be in 2020. It gave us time to prep and position the brand ourselves as the new leaders of the business. The outcome of that meeting was that information would be shared and the business would be valued so that the option of an MBO could be explored.

My inside voice wasn't calling the Founder bonkers on this occasion - my inside voice was weighing up whether I wanted to do this myself or in partnership? Who do I speak to so I can get the funding? How does an MBO even work?

There was no question around whether I would be able to do it, and even if there was, we had the best part of two years to get our ducks in a row and make it happen!

Over the next few months, things progressed slowly. The valuation came back and I had made my decision. If I was going to buy this business, I needed to take 100% responsibility. I needed to do it by myself. My life had improved in so many areas because I had stopped waiting for someone else to fix things, and because I had stopped refusing to take responsibility for things. If I wanted the confidence to know I was going to make the right decision and have a successful outcome, I needed to commit with 100% responsibility.

I can do this. And there's still plenty of time for me to sort out the bits I'm not quite sure about. It's only 2018 - we're talking 2020 before this happens. Things could not be better!

Fierce And Driven
By the time we got to October 2018, there was a weird shift. We all knew what we were doing, and where we were heading but I think when you make a decision like that, a switch flicks. I had autonomy in the business, but it still wasn't mine and I was both mindful and respectful of that.

The Founder wanted me to feel like it was mine already and these two things together, although they sound like they should work, in reality, created a strange disconnect.

I was ready and I didn't want to wait until 2020. In fact, if we were going to do this, I wanted to do it now or not at all. I had never been so sure of myself. This was happening and I still hadn't even secured the money! So I pushed myself to have the difficult conversation - to speak to this person who was offering me something I'd written down as a dream and tell them, "Yes please, now please." Even with all that growth, it was massively alien to me.

That conversation began the proceedings of an MBO. Heads of terms were signed and agreed. Prior to this I thought HOTS was an American term for when someone takes a fancy to someone else! We negotiated a price - that was tough and took more than a few courageous conversations, not only with the Founder but also with my investor (aka my father)! This was the first time I had to properly draw a line between business and personal. I had to look after myself and my own interests first, and I really had to stand up for myself and defend my confidence in my abilities.

I learnt so much about myself in this process, I almost scared myself at times. Somewhere along the line I had become genuinely fierce, I had become driven, I knew what I wanted and how to make it a success, and my faith in my business acumen was unquestionable.

On Monday 1st April 2019, I got into my car and instead of driving to the office, I went to meet the Founder to sign contracts and become the Owner of Green Umbrella Marketing. I remember driving on autopilot, parking and just sitting there for a minute.

Have I really done this? Have I really convinced someone that I'm worthy of taking their legacy forward? Secured investment, built a team who supports me in what I'm going to do, and have peers who are excited for me?

Am I really about to do this? Me - that person who has given up so many times in the past. Me - who spent so long letting the world just happen to her. The answer was yes.

Can I really do this? Yes. Because that's not who I am anymore. I've grown this much already, and I'm still growing and will continue to grow.

I got out of the car, signed a contract, made a bank transfer and went about my day.

I was now the proud Owner of Green Umbrella Marketing.

Change Your Dialogue
Remember when I described waking up from that surgery?

Instead of talking about physical pain, read it once again but this time imagine I'm talking about emotional or spiritual pain. Imagine that the pain I'm talking about is the thing that is stopping you from growing right now.

For years, the physical pain had screamed above the numbness. I had accepted and lived daily with the pain for a long time - and I mean years before I asked for help or did anything to change the situation. In fact, I'd go and do things that I knew would aggravate my pain because I didn't want to miss out on things.

I had no idea just how limited I had become or how much I had been compensating just so I could continue to survive the other challenges I had been facing and also complete the most basic tasks. I was unaware, I was blind to it and so every day I was just reliving and reliving that same pain.

That's where I was, in all areas of my life. Drifting in constant pain, consumed by it and with no direction. Whatever your situation, just living isn't enough. If you've had challenges and experiences that you've had to endure, I am sorry. But now it's time to put those things to pasture. Living and reliving it every day must become unacceptable for you to start your growth journey.

Remember when I described that thought I had, sitting on my bed in tears?

Life doesn't have to be this way.

That's the moment I took responsibility for my life, opened my eyes and ears to the possibilities around me, made a plan and stuck to it. If you want to grow, it's time for you to change the dialogue and choose who and what you want to be.

Just remember, I didn't go from there to here overnight, and it's probable (but not impossible) that it will take time for you too. I had to recognise and take responsibility for the behaviours that were holding me back and commit to changing them, however simple or complex that might be. I had to be vulnerable enough to identify where I could be better and then do something about it.

I just want to say one last thing, my growth is far from complete - I am far from done! Sometimes, when it comes to making change, you are all you need. Sometimes you need to ask for help. Even with everything I have shared with you here, it's important you understand that I was still not wise enough to ask for help until very recently.

Growth is a lifelong commitment, it's the best and most rewarding commitment you can ever make.

About Me

I'm the employee turned business owner who has been gifted with the title of entrepreneur by my peers. I'm a blogger, podcaster, public speaker, and winner of multiple awards; a daughter, sister, wife, mother, and grandmother.

I'm the success story who grew up with a difficult background. I left home too early, dropped out of education (twice), had kids too early, endured toxic relationships, neglected my mental health - I drifted through life before I realised it wasn't too late to take control... And wow am I glad that I did!

In 2013, I found where I was supposed to be in the world and since then I have been working with small business owners to launch, develop and perfect their online presence. I'm known for my cool, calm approach to digital marketing and my ability to leave every audience walking away with practical strategies that can be implemented immediately into their businesses.

Today I'm the proud MD of Green Umbrella Marketing, a successful, UK based, digital marketing agency known for providing outsourced social media management, marketing mentorship and coaching, as well as design and print services. From being lost and rudderless I have grown and become an all-around fountain of wisdom when it comes to online marketing strategies. I exist in a fast-moving world, and I love it!

I'm driven by the fact that in today's world, it doesn't matter how big or small your business or marketing budget is, you can be a major player in your market.

But most of all, I'm an advocate for success and for anyone that not only dares to dream bigger but is ready to take the steps required to make it happen for themselves.

And if that sounds like you… then I'm dedicating this chapter to you in celebration of all the successes that are just around the corner for you. I believe in you.

Your Dreams Are Valid

Rebecca Hocking
Owner
RH Cakes and Bake Along With Bec

"Everyone needs to be valued. Everyone has the potential to give something back" -- Princess Diana

Don't you hate that society has our life all mapped out for us? Finish school, go to college, go to university, get a good job, meet the perfect man, get married, have a child, be the perfect housewife and mother. And if you could do it in that order too, that would be great!

Looking back I guess I didn't want to conform to what was "expected" of me, even at a young age! I didn't want to follow the obvious path.

Despite being very good academically and getting the grades, when I reached 16 I knew I didn't want to stay in full-time education. While I didn't really know what I wanted to be, I knew that the college and university route was not the path I wanted to take. I didn't want to study anymore and certainly didn't crave university life.

My mother, like most parents, put her foot down and said that I needed to find a full-time job if I didn't want to go to college. So, in order to stop my mum from nagging me, I searched for jobs AND signed up to a college course on business administration and finance.

185

Two weeks later, I found a job as a full-time office junior in a firm of solicitors. Was it exciting? Nope! Photocopying, filing and the numerous trips to the shop to buy tea, coffee, milk and of course, Dunhills for the boss, was not how I wanted to spend my time.

Was it paying me well? This was long before the days of minimum wage and I think it was £60 for a 40 hour week.

Was it what I wanted? At that time, yes absolutely. I was independent with no real clue about the world and wanted to be an employed person. I wanted to be treated as an adult because that's fun, right?

I spent the next few years working in the legal environment, progressing to a legal receptionist, secretary and finally, a paralegal. I even went back to that place I had been so adamant to avoid - university - and obtained a law degree.

I wore a suit to work, did the 9-5, and court rooms, barristers chambers and tribunals became my life. When you say you work in law, people are genuinely impressed. They immediately think: high salary, easy job, lavish lifestyle.

Nothing could be further from the truth. The salary isn't always high, the job is rarely that easy and the lifestyle is rather exhausting. But against the odds, it would seem that my career was all mapped out. I had grown into the legal profession and was working my way up the ladder.

Roaring 20s...?

Unlike many people, my 20s is the decade of my life that I tend not to reminisce about that much. The time in my life when I made bad choices and built toxic relationships with people who damaged my confidence, self-esteem and worth. Strained family relationships, and being overworked and underpaid (among other things), was detrimental to my wellbeing.

But it wasn't all bad. There were definitely fun times. I recall travelling to London to receive a prestigious award presented by Cherie Blair (the former prime minister's wife), on behalf of my boss! There were about 250 city lawyers and barristers and the whole thing was broadcast on the BBC.

And then an unforeseen event ended up being a turning point in how I viewed my life, relationships and career.

A woman called Sian joined our law firm and we instantly got on. She was a vibrant young lady who worked hard and had a personality larger than life - not only a brilliant legal professional, but a certified party girl who became a very good friend of mine. I remember her coming to a fancy dress party dressed as Tinkerbell and from then on, that nickname always stuck.

And then I got a shocking phone call. Sian had gone. I could make no sense of it. She had been out shopping and collapsed, sadly suffering a brain hemorrhage and passing away. She had been in her early 30s with everything to live for and she had gone. I still find this hard to think about even today. The unfair cards that life deals to people.

When something like this happens, you instantly start questioning everything. What am I doing? Is this what life is really all about? Is law for me? But this is all I know…

Coupled with a relationship breakdown completely out of the blue, I began a period of my life where I didn't know what I wanted and what purpose I really had anymore. I only knew two things for sure: I definitely didn't want to work in law and I definitely didn't want another relationship! Well, one of those things still remains true, and the other… I've been happily married for 10 years.

Courtrooms To Cupcakes

By now you're probably thinking, "What the hell? How do cakes fit into all this?" So I am going to fast forward several years to when I found a whisk in my hand and never looked back.

People close to me will know that I've never been much of a culinary wizard. The only recipe book in my flat was a takeaway menu, and I would avoid cooking if I possibly could. I wasn't really one for hobbies either. Then one day, I saw an advert on TV about a cake decorating magazine, and I found myself turning to my partner and saying, "I'm going to have a go at that."

A few weeks later, friends of ours had a baby and I remembered seeing a baby blocks cake in the magazine that would be perfect for the occasion, so I set out to make it for them. Everything was made from scratch and looking back, the result wasn't that great. But you know what? I absolutely loved making it! More than that, I loved their reaction when they received it. They were truly touched and I felt so proud that I had gone way outside my comfort zone.

That reaction to the cake lit a fire in me. I had made them happy with something I had created. It was a feeling I cannot explain and a feeling I still get to this day when I deliver celebration cakes for people. This couple is still a customer of mine and I have made numerous cakes for their child, Gethin, for a number of years now.

With a new hobby that I enjoyed, I spent every spare minute flipping through recipe books. I'd spend a few hours a week playfully testing new ideas, baking and creating animals and flowers out of icing.

In September 2012, my mum came across a baking competition at the Malvern Autumn Show and encouraged me to enter. At that time, baking was just a hobby to me but my husband and I had planned to go to the show anyway, so why not enter it! What did I have to lose?

When we got to the show, I was met by my mother outside the competition tent where the winning cakes were displayed inside. I swear she had been crying and looked a bit shaken.

She said, "You had better go and have a look." Oh great, now I was nervous. I must have crashed and burned and made myself look ridiculous in front of the celebrity judge, Jean Christophe Novelli.

I walked in and scanned the room. Omg, I couldn't believe it! The card next to my cake read: 'Best in Show'. It was a definite pinch-me moment. Here I was just a few months into baking, an ex-paralegal who could burn water, and a professional chef had just awarded me!

That was the real beginning of my story and where my life was going to take me. Over the next nine years, I built up a highly successful cake business, supplying many local eateries and had customers across the UK. I made numerous cakes for all sorts of occasions and even won a few more awards. I had grown from a hobby baker to a successful businesswoman. I had "made it".

What could go wrong?

The 2020 Effect
The Covid-19 pandemic was something that no one saw coming and nobody could have planned for. I was forced to close my business for over three months. This time was full of uncertainty and financial worry - how could this happen?

Our whole way of life had changed overnight - we couldn't socialise, certainly couldn't have parties, and weddings were cancelled. My confidence had taken a massive hit and I could not see how my business would recover. I genuinely didn't feel as though I had the energy to start again and rebuild my business - the business I had slaved night and day to build up. I genuinely believed this was the end and that I would have to get a "proper job".

Several weeks into the first lockdown, I had gone from working six days a week to doing nothing, and the boredom was starting to get to me. I had to do something! I thought about doing a live bake along on my business page, just something to pass the time and maybe help parents and children who were also going stir crazy in lockdown. I did a few sessions and I couldn't believe that people actually joined in, messaging me to say how much they loved it and sending me photos of their completed bakes. I had a feeling of purpose again. It wasn't making me any money of course, but it felt good and I started to enjoy myself again.

I was inspired to explore this direction some more and developed Bake Along With Bec, a children's membership group and subscription box. Each month, kids would receive a recipe card, piece of equipment and all the ingredients they needed delivered to their door. They could then stream my instructional videos on how to make their cakes and bake along with me.

I launched the box, with no real idea what I was doing but knew I had a passion for it. Teaching children to bake and learn a new skill was fulfilling something in me on a level I had not felt before, and I soon had a loyal membership.

Eventually, the lockdowns and restrictions were lifted and lives returned to normal. I was able to reopen my business and quickly discovered that my business could recover from the pandemic. I didn't have to go through sleepless nights or question the sustainability of my business because it went back to the way it was before the pandemic hit.

But what about the bake along? I had started it as something to do but then found that I wanted to continue doing it. I had parents telling me their children looked forward to the delivery each month and my inbox was always full of photos of happy children with their bakes. So I made a brave decision to keep going with my second business. I didn't really know what would happen and whether the novelty of the box would wear off for people but I knew I wanted to try. I didn't want to give up on something I found so rewarding.

Fast forward to today, nearly two years on, and I am still developing the box and membership. It is definitely a learning curve, as elements of this business are alien to me, but I am prepared to give it my all. I am proud that I have some members with me who have been there since the very start. I have older members that have told me that I have inspired them to start their own baking journeys too.

The fact that I have had such an impact so early on in my venture is incredible and these young people are one of the reasons I am determined not to give up. I need to do this, not only for myself but for each of them as well.

I have to juggle both businesses which is sometimes challenging but I made the decision that I shouldn't give up on something that I am passionate about. Something that feels as though I'm giving something back.

Inspiring The Future With My Empire

When I look back at my childhood and my schooling, baking and cooking was never a priority. I think the level of my cooking classes at school consisted of Angel Crunch (Angel Delight with crushed up digestives!). I mean, is that actually a thing? It's not a recipe I have cracked out at a dinner party since, that's for sure!

Having researched the situation in the current climate, there still isn't a huge amount of culinary literacy in the curriculum and I think this is such a shame. I believe baking develops so many skills in children. It also encourages family time and is an escape from the technology-based world we have all become so reliant on. There aren't a lot of young people who leave school thinking, "Hmm, I want to be a cake maker!" and I would love to change that.

Education seems to place so much emphasis on certain careers and paths for young people to follow. I am not saying that we shouldn't encourage children to do well at school. But, what about the people who are not academically inclined or don't want the 9-5 life? What about the people who want to follow an alternative passion or dream?

I gave up on a career in law, a career that can set you up for life. I tell people this and they think I am insane. But eventually, I ended up doing what I loved and not what was expected of me. You will have self-doubt, to be totally truthful I still do, but if the pandemic has taught me anything, it is that none of us know what is around the corner.

We are all guilty of saying, "I will do that one day", but what if that day never comes? What if we waste another day, another week with that attitude. Life can change in an instant and we should grab opportunities wherever they arise.

I truly believe that self-development never ends and we can always grow as a person. During 2021, I came across the Queens In Business Club. And although I didn't feel like I belonged at first (I was just a cake maker among women who had changed lives), now, I am beginning to see that I have a lot in common with the Co-Founders and members of this group.

I am a female business owner striving to grow and be the best version of myself. I have spent years having my ability knocked and feeling like I wasn't good enough. But my growth as a person is slowly changing. I *do* have products and services that people want to buy. I *do* have products that give joy and services that help children grow. For that, I should be proud.

It may be a different empire to others, but it's my empire.

If you had said to me, even just 12 months ago, that I would be writing this chapter and putting all these words on paper, I would have laughed at you. Even now, I still second guess myself at times, wondering whether what I'm doing is enough.

If there is one thing I could tell my younger self, it would be to have confidence. You are good enough and don't let anyone tell you otherwise . If you are reading this chapter and are thinking of starting a business or beginning a new journey as an entrepreneur, never give up on your passion. If my journey has taught me anything, it is that perhaps the obvious choice isn't the correct one for you.

I am a true believer that everything happens for a reason. If I didn't go through the challenges that I went through to get here today, I would have been stuck following the law route and would be spending my days in a horsehair wig, fighting the good fight. Clearly, that wasn't my destiny and I couldn't be happier.

I'm just an ordinary woman, from an ordinary background, doing an ordinary job. But no one can take away the things I have learned and what I have achieved. We all have something to give to others, so go out there and give it. It probably won't be an easy ride, but it will be worthwhile and rewarding. Live your life how you want to, do what makes you happy and more importantly, believe in yourself.

About Me

I am Bec aka Rebecca and as the owner of RH Cakes and Bake Along With Bec, am often known as 'The Cake Lady'.

I have lived my whole life in South Wales and now reside in Caerphilly with husband, dog and our six ducks (yes, you read that right!).

My early career was in the legal field but I swapped the legal scales for weighing scales when I discovered that perhaps the obvious choice wasn't the correct one. I am a multi-award winning cake maker who had a successful business prior to the Covid-19 pandemic which I thought would not recover. Thankfully, I was wrong, and the pandemic gave me an opportunity to start another business and discover a passion that I didn't even know that I had. So now I also teach and encourage kids to learn the skill of baking!

In 2021, I stumbled across the Queens In Business Club and I liken it to getting on a train and getting off at the wrong platform, only to find that the destination you arrived at is far better than the original place you were heading to. I am truly honoured to be a part of this book with such incredible ladies and I hope that readers will see that even though we are all from such different backgrounds, we all share the same attributes and inspirations. I certainly couldn't have written this chapter without their encouragement and support. Thank you for believing in me.

I have to give a mention to my mother who made me determined to get a job at 16 and not go to university - and also for suggesting I enter my first baking competition. And to my husband Simon, as I could not do what I do without his love, support and encouragement - maybe he will believe me now it's in print!

I dedicate this chapter to all the people that think if you're "ordinary" you can't succeed. I hope I can prove to you that you can.

Overcoming Adversities

Thelma Foreman
Travel Business Owner
Inspiretoinspired

"Faith is taking the first step even when you don't see the full staircase" – Dr. Martin Luther King

The fear of rejection can run deep. So deep that it can stop us from progressing forward. That fear has been a part of me for a very long time, manifesting itself in many different ways. It doesn't matter how surface-level the fear is, I always feel it in my core. It has been a stumbling block for me for many years.

I didn't realise how much it was taking a toll on my mental health until I turned 16. I couldn't understand why I felt so devastated all the time and often found myself asking, why me Lord? I had been in the care of my grandmother (or Mama as I called her) and apart from my siblings since three years old. But the effects of that only hit me later. I guess I was too small to understand what was going on.

I was quite a timid child. I can never forget this particular day at school when I asked my teacher if I could be excused from class to use the toilet. For some reason, she said "no" and sent me back to my seat. I didn't want to talk back because I was taught to obey adults, so I walked back to my seat, and then I wet myself.

As soon as I got home, I told Mama (my grandmother) what happened. She asked me to point out which teacher had done this to me, so I waited by the doorway until I saw her. Then I ran back into the house and pointed out the door, "Mama, the teacher is coming! That one, in the middle!"

Mama called her over and I was so scared that I ran into the next room. But I wanted to hear what they would say. So I laid down on the floor and pressed my ear next to the gap at the bottom of the door. I could hear Mama shouting - she was a fierce lady and always expressed her thoughts freely. I can't remember how my teacher responded but the next day at school, I felt rejected by her. This carried on for the rest of the school year and it made me even more timid. I had a hard time learning after that.

Many children encounter moments of rejection throughout their lives. And when it comes from your peers, it can be even more heartbreaking. In eighth grade, the class prefect was asked to check the students' attire. Everyone stood up quickly to fix their uniforms, afraid to be marked down on their school record. I felt so powerless as I desperately tried to neaten up my uniform. As the prefect approached me, our eyes met and I felt my heart leap out of my chest. I wanted to pass the inspection, but unfortunately she wrote my name down on the list. I felt so let down by my own classmate. Another moment of rejection.

Fast forward to my adult life, those childhood moments find themselves popping back up from time to time. I was training as a machine embroiderer, and the class started sharing stories. Being quite shy, I had to muster up the courage to share a motivational quote I liked. As I started speaking, a young lady cut me off for not pronouncing some of the words right. I felt like my good intentions were turned into an uncalled for embarrassment. I felt ashamed and awkward for the rest of the day.

I hate to say it but I let that moment replay in my mind for months afterwards. Slowly but surely, I learned to let go of these hurtful remarks, because if you're not careful, you can carry shame around with you for the rest of your life. Luckily, I managed to continue with grace and dignity, leaving all the bad memories behind.

Finding My Feet

After I received my machine embroidery training, I started to look for a job. I applied to every posting that would suit my skills but no luck. I got so frustrated going into town for interviews all the time, spending all my money on bus fares instead of buying groceries to nourish my tired body.

Eventually, I shared the difficulties with my friends and one of them introduced me to a lady named Maggie who could put me in touch with an employment agency. I was delighted by all the new positions that were available and sent in my applications.

It took several more weeks before I was finally offered a position that I liked. I started to imagine what I would buy with my first paycheck - I must get myself some goodies. But before I started, I had to sign a contract with Maggie, agreeing to give her a percentage of my wage. Honestly, I had no idea that I was supposed to pay for this service.

I started work the following Monday and I was overjoyed to finally have a job. I made sure to arrive extra early because I wanted to make a good impression. I sat outside the premises, waiting for work to begin. I could tell that it was a wealthy neighbourhood because the houses were so beautiful and big.

Finally, it was time to begin. The other workers took their places but I had a small orientation to complete before I could start. During the discussion with my new boss, I realised that she was looking for a very experienced dressmaker and needed skills that I didn't have yet. I told her I was capable of the basics and that I could prove myself to be a quick learner. But she seemed very annoyed that I didn't meet her criteria. I think the only reason I was allowed to stay was because she was in desperate need of help and didn't have time to find someone new.

Then I got to the sewing room. Oh dear... I wasn't expecting to see industrial machines. The only machines I had used were domestic ones. I tried to get on with my task and figure out how industrial machines worked but they were quite fast and scary. I was worried I was going to trap my fingers and the nervousness took over.

That's when my boss started shouting, angry that she'd asked for a skilled worker and received me instead. Suddenly, the atmosphere in the room was very tense and quiet. No one spoke a word but I could see them glancing over at me from time to time. I felt ashamed for the rest of the day.

I left work with a heavy heart and cried all the way to the bus stop. I was so angry with myself and hurt by the occurrence of another rejection. I didn't like the way my boss had spoken to me in front of everyone, like I was a child being told off. I didn't want to work in an environment like that. I told myself that if I ever had employees of my own in the future, I would treat them with much more respect than I had been given.

The next day, I informed Maggie about what had happened and told her I wasn't going back. She found another position for me, where I was lucky enough to be trained by a kind woman who encouraged me to progress. I was happy there for two years and eventually felt confident enough to consider starting up my own business.

A Wish To The Universe

In 1999, I migrated to London. And although I had dreams of studying fashion design, I ended up in the health sector. Although it wasn't what I had envisioned for myself, I loved caring for people. But my dream of becoming a business owner didn't go away. I wanted the freedom that came with it, to be there for my new family and have enough money to travel the world.

So I sent my wish out into the universe.

One day, I stumbled across an amazing opportunity to join a network marketing business. I hadn't heard of networking marketing before but I could see how it aligned with my vision for the future. And most importantly, it would give me the freedom and finances to live out my dream.

The role involved selling a product to help adventurers travel more for less. And in doing so, I would get to travel and be paid for it too! I thought it would be an easy sell, but I was so wrong…

The following months were stressful. People were excited by the offer at first but in order to benefit they had to onboard someone onto the team too and they didn't want the hassle that comes with that. I think they were afraid of rejection and of not being able to sell to people. I hold my hands up, I used to be like that too and had my fair share of rejection in this new venture.

I tried to sell the product to my close friends. I thought they'd be up for it because it would give them the ideal lifestyle we all deserve. But they weren't in the right mindset to take this on. Even though I wanted this so badly for them.

I had to learn to let them follow their own path and I moved on to connecting with other, more like-minded people. People who wanted to build an empire like me.

I learnt a lot about myself during this time. I thought about what motivates me, what my vision is and what my purpose is. Who are the people I am meant to serve and why? Personal growth is a continuous process and never a quick fix. It takes a lot of energy and self-belief to keep improving.

I'm on a mission of progression and finding this network marketing opportunity has given me unlimited potential to expand in so many ways. But most of all, I realised that I have to love myself in order to grow. I had to learn to process my emotions and let go of situations and feelings that don't serve me. It's about acceptance.

I have learned to resolve challenges in my business in a healthy way, not taking rejections too seriously and understanding that potential clients may say "no" at times but perhaps they aren't the right fit for me.

Learning how to accept was my hidden power.

Sometimes you might feel like you are rejected for whatever circumstances you are facing - it can be from family, partners, friends, neighbours or work colleagues. You have to recognise the reason why you are feeling rejected and take time to process your emotions.

It can be frustrating when you feel your work is not appreciated but persevere and be positive. Continue to be you and at some point your hard work will be seen.

It took me a while to believe that it was worth a few nos to finally get to the YES! My love for the business and the fact that I can help change many lives keeps me patient and I have faith knowing that I'm serving others in a meaningful way. There will be times when challenges arise but I learned how to persevere with courage. I have built a mindset to conquer and I am in charge of how I want to live my life.

We all have unique gifts and talents that can serve others in different ways. I choose to continue my network marketing business. I am proud to have changed many lives for the better and give ordinary people like me the opportunity to build an abundance of wealth and become the best versions of themselves.

Don't surrender to giving up after facing rejections in your life. Think of rejection as a pulling force that gets you closer and closer to where your passion lies and where you are truly meant to be.

About Me

Hailing from the hills of Grant's Town, St Mary, Jamaica and living in London since 1999, I have three children - my son, 36 years and my daughters, 16 and 18 years.

I established myself as a machine embroiderer and dressmaker, following in the footsteps of my grandmother who brought me up. Although sewing garments wasn't my ideal choice at first, I was very delighted I gave it a chance because I found it to be very creative and I received some great encouragement and appraisal from my customers.

After training as a machine embroiderer, I had dreams of studying fashion design in London or France, but I ended up in health and social care when I migrated to the UK. I did enjoy working as a health care assistant, support worker and rehabilitation assistant but I'm always looking to learn new things and have fun - I classify myself as the fun queen!

I'm a go-getter and live my life of faith, following my path and adapting to changes. I am always on a journey of

206

transformation. Life is a process and I'm living it to the best of my ability.

Thank you so much Queens In Business for this amazing and empowering community for female entrepreneurs. I am the change.

Finding Your Gift

Mariana Diaz Mancera

CEO, Entrepreneur Architect and Brand Director,
SPACIO Architects LTD and CREE, CONFIA, CRECE

"The meaning of life is to find your gift, the purpose of life is to give it away" -- Pablo Picasso

Many people spend their lives trying to find happiness, dancing on water looking for some certainty, clarity and guidance. Basically, trying to find a way of living with a purpose!

I have been one of those many people, until one random rainy evening in September 2021, a wave of clarity swept over me. I was in the car and I heard a wise quote from Pablo Picasso on the radio: "The secret of life is to find your gift. The purpose of life is to give it away."

Suddenly, I realised I had a gift and I had been using it since I was a child. This realisation was the turning point of it all. It was one of the biggest personal and professional growths that took place in my entire life. I had found my purpose.

But what is your gift, Mariana, you might be wondering… Bear with me, as we all know there are no shortcuts in life. I promise you will find out before this chapter ends, and hopefully, my story can also help you unleash your full potential and find your own gift.

It all started during the sunny summers in Estepona, Costa del Sol, Spain. My first steps as an entrepreneur. I was eight years old when I was working on a creative project with my friends. We were making beautiful, thread bracelets and selling them at the beach residential complex. It was a success! I don't recall doing any bookkeeping, but it was the only entrepreneurial adventure I had before I reached my adult life.

I had a happy childhood. I have lovely memories of our big family events and fun birthday parties. I have 41 cousins - something that comes as a surprise to most people. I loved socialising and being in the street playing football, skating, practising athletics or attending piano lessons. I have always been willing to learn and improve. Dad was working full-time to provide for us while mum was at home looking after us three girls, with me being the eldest.

I had a "normal" childhood with supportive parents who encouraged me to study and gain qualifications for a profession that I could rely on. This is actually still a dream for many people in Spain. A lot of people pursue certainty at work over freedom. Maybe because of the lack of business education. I was never taught that there was an alternative path to build a career or start a business.

It's curious that even my dad, who was running his own construction business with his two brothers, advised me that the best thing for me to do was to get a job as a civil servant. He thought that that path would set me up for life, working from 9am to 2pm, giving me enough time to spend with my family.

As you will soon realise, I did not quite agree with that.

Difficult Decisions

I have always known that investing in myself and my education would bring me happiness, joy and success in life. I remember a conversation I had with my mum at the age of 16 about what I wanted to be and what I wanted to study in order to achieve that. I told her that I liked the idea of being an architect, to design and build people's houses, or maybe a psychologist to be able to help people with challenges in their lives. I have always loved listening to others and my friends always come to me for advice.

My mum came up with a great plan, she asked me, "Why don't you do both? You can pick architecture as a career, and by nature, you will genuinely be helping people along the way."

Voilá! Every time I speak to my mum, she always has the most fitting answer to my concerns. Answers that I bought into very easily. And there I was, asking my parents if I could move to Granada, a city one and a half hours away from my home, because I couldn't study architecture in my hometown, Málaga.

The truth is though, I felt I did not belong in Málaga. I needed to escape to find where I fit in this world. I remember being surrounded by feelings of jealousy, envy, competition, among other things. As a young girl with not enough knowledge and tools to overcome these feelings, I knew I had to find a place where I could be the best version of myself.

Twenty years later, I still find myself feeling those unpleasant emotions from time to time. But now I am able to confront these emotions without going as far as moving away!

At the age of 23, I moved from Granada to Northern Italy, only this time I was not running away. I applied to the Erasmus program to study architecture for a year. I love getting to know different cultures and learning how to speak different languages.

In 2012, at the age of twenty seven, I moved back home after graduating in Spain. My life as an architect did not start smoothly. Spain still hadn't recovered from its financial crisis, which started in 2008. Salaries were very low, and most importantly, I lacked motivation.

I found myself at another decisive moment in my life. And I found myself moving to the UK with the hope of finding my 9 to 5 dream job.

I remember it as if it just happened yesterday. A cold and white 15th of November, landing in the big city with my boyfriend at the time, who joined me in this new and exciting life adventure. We had the best opportunity ever - we even had free lodging for one whole month! Little did I know that I was about to experience a massive challenge.

Although I did not know it at the time, overcoming a life challenge leads to a growth spurt. But you have to make major life decisions and accept big changes to get there. That is how we grow. Have you ever thought about this process before?

Follow the diagram and think about:

- A challenge you have experienced in the past
- The decision you took to overcome that challenge
- The change that decision created in your life
- How long it took you to accept the change
- Finally after the acceptance, how good you felt about growing from that situation

To my surprise, it was not as easy as I thought it would be to find myself a position in an architectural office in London. My spoken English was not that fluent and there were less job

212

opportunities at that time. I spent almost two years trying to build my confidence with the language by working with kids, both as a nanny and as a private Spanish teacher. I cannot lie, it was tough. I wanted to work as an architect but instead I found myself pushing a baby in a buggy. She was adorable, though!

Eventually, I finally landed my dream job as an architect, and I was so excited! But you know what? Only four months later, I began to feel unhappy. It was at that moment I realised that my real dream was not to get my dream job but to be able to find a flexible working lifestyle that allowed me to create a family, spend quality time with my loved ones back in Spain, and still have a professional career. I used to daydream about this and even shared some potential business ideas with some friends.

Sharing My Vision

Summer 2015, I got a phone call from one of my best friends back in Spain talking about this network marketing business opportunity that was giving her great results. I was looking for a way to make extra income to be able to quit my 9 to 5 job as an architect employee and start my own online architecture business, and this opportunity was the answer! It was clear to me. I felt this was going to be the key that would allow me to enjoy life with my family and friends while working with my passion, architecture.

I had no clue how to do the business - but my 'why' was BIG, and I trusted my heart and gave it my best. For the first time in one and a half years, I used my hour-long commute for my online business, and my thirty-minute lunch breaks to share the business opportunity on WhatsApp, video calls and also used those spare minutes to arrange after work dinners with my London based connections.

It was hard, and I often found myself in tears. I had little support from my family or friends, and I found it hard to sell the business opportunity in the UK. Most of my team ended up being from Spain and very far away. No one understood why an architect would want to get involved in network marketing! I had no one to share my vision with during that time. I just wanted to find a balance between my professional and personal life. I wanted to be a mum one day and be able to have a career while still staying at home to look after my own kids.

I asked myself often if I was investing all this time in the right business and I found myself feeling unsure. For three months during the summer of 2016, I even stopped sharing the business opportunity with others. And funnily enough, it was at that moment that I realised the power of passive income and thought that things could really work out if I just put in the effort. So I decided to follow my gut instinct and continue with the business. I believed in myself so I was determined to trust that business model and grow my side income. I had a plan, although it was not written, it was in my heart!

2017 was a transformational year for me, and although I was definitely becoming a better version of myself, I still had to go through some difficult situations. I had accepted that my happiness started with letting go of toxic relationships. And unfortunately, that involved not only some of my friends but also my partner for the last 8 years.

I quit my job as an architect employee and thanks to the extra income I was generating monthly with my network marketing business, I felt comfortable in making this decision. I had earned enough money and courage to believe in myself and to start my own online architecture firm, SPACIO architects. It has been the most amazing, but also stressful, years of my life. Building up a traditional business that was growing rapidly with a lot of projects on board, converting myself into a boss for many others when I only wanted to be a boss to myself.

Even with this achievement, I chose not to quit my online business but continued planting seeds in it. I never stopped sharing the business opportunity with everyone. This allowed me, back in October 2019, to stop accepting as many architecture projects and just focus on a few projects that I loved with the clients that I really liked.

To hold me accountable, I recorded myself sharing my goals and dreams of when I first started my online business, and I DID IT. I am now free to travel wherever I want and continue working from a laptop or a smartphone. I always encourage my team to share their 'why' and goals with others because it can help you feel committed and motivated to persevere until you achieve it.

I hit a big milestone within the company becoming Brand Director and got recognised as an Inspirational Leader in the UK in April 2020.

Then Covid-19 hit the world. Luckily, as I had an online business, I continued to grow a big community in many different countries and I loved every minute I spent working with my team.

After all, I had found a business model that supported my ambition and passion to transform people's lives with zero risks. My vision aligned with the company's core values and I found a business model that was an excellent driver for people to get started on their own leadership and entrepreneurial paths. And on top of this, I was now having full support of close friends and especially, from whom soon became my fiancé, and now also the father of my daughter.

This business did not require financial investment but did require my time, health and resilience - I am resilient, I have always been. But I never made my health a priority...

"Yes, I can!"
"Yes, of course!"
"Yes, sure!"

Have you ever uttered these words to:

- Your clients, when they text you late in the evenings, asking for an extra piece of work?

- Your business partner, when they ask you to do something they could actually do themselves?

- Your friend or family member, when they ask you to do work as a favour or request it at a discounted price?

- Yourself, when you find yourself working extra hours on weekdays and weekends?

To me, saying these words brought me stress, discomfort, anxiety, uncertainty and illness quite often. Learning how to do business, while keeping myself healthy has been one of my biggest lessons in my entrepreneurial journey and is something I need to be checking on regularly even now.

Asking For Help

Not only was I working countless hours, I was also feeling very lonely. There were no entrepreneurs around me who could empathise with my difficulties. All of my friends were working as employees and could not really understand what I had envisioned.

I had two businesses running successfully and I was overwhelmed. I didn't have a written business plan. I did everything by following my heart.

I knew I needed help and that summer of 2019, I was finally ready to ask for it. I went to a free business event in London, which completely changed the direction of my entrepreneurial journey. I finally found the business community of like-minded people who understood me! I was feeling positive and empowered. I wanted to take my businesses to the next level, and that required a new mindset, which required new learning. I started to understand that entrepreneurship, in itself, was a journey. Not a destination.

I feel immensely grateful to myself for having said YES to my heart seven years ago. I feel grateful to my whole team, uplines, downlines and crosslines. Everything I teach is based on what I learned from others and my own failures and successes.

I have a message of hope for everyone reading this right now. While this is still an uncertain and difficult time, we can still find positivity in it. We have a chance to learn and adapt to new ways of working and living - something I believe will continue long after this is over.

My Wish And My 'Why'
I never thought I would be starting my entrepreneurial journey in a foreign country but I did it! That just proves how unpredictable and surprising life is. You might be in a similar position yourself right now, feeling like you are not living the life that you deserve and thinking that you might be feeling that way for the rest of your life. Or maybe you went as far as setting yourself goals in order to achieve that dream life you had in mind but feel like you are not making any real progress.

I understand, as I have been in that exact situation before. From my experience, we end up feeling stuck only when we don't have certainty - when we do not know where we want to go or what we want to achieve. We sometimes hurriedly set goals without a semblance of confidence in ourselves and as a result, we give up.

I always make it a point to make my team understand that you have to find that burning desire that makes you want to turn dreams into action, so you don't end up giving up.

Your goal not only has to be S.M.A.R.T. (Specific, Measurable, Achievable, Relevant and Time-bound), but, in my experience, you also have to be emotionally invested in it.

And how do you link emotions with goals?

You can link them by refraining from asking yourself what you want and where you want to be, but *why* you want that certain thing.

I ask myself *why*? I ask myself this numerous times until my true desire exposes itself to me. The 'why' that is emotionally relevant to me. And that is what makes me get up in the morning and work tirelessly to achieve my dreams.

My initial wish was to be able to create my own online architecture firm in the UK. But...

Why? Because I wanted my own financial freedom

Why? Because I wanted to be able to create a family and still be able to work from home.

Why? Because that is what my mum did not get to have, and always wanted for her children.

As you can see, if you continue asking yourself 'why?', you will get to the real wish - one that is very close to your heart.

The Only Way Is Up
October 2020, the month we had planned to celebrate our big day in Spain. Covid-19's second wave hit the UK badly. We could not fly to Spain to get married and countries were putting further entry restrictions up. I was in my late thirties and my fiancé was in his early forties. So we decided to make good use of the time and create a family in this pandemic period. It was a great idea, why not?

It was, indeed. But in order to achieve that, I had to live with the most vulnerable version of myself for the whole year. Pregnancy was a tough time for me. I was emotionally very unstable, I lost my strength, I felt lonely even though I had the best support ever from my other half at home. I went from being "me" to "us", from 25th June 2021, when I met the love of my life, my daughter, Pia.

I was in an emotional state that words could not describe, and I am sure that if you are a mum, you don't need any further words from me to describe how overwhelmed I felt during those times. Stress, fears, anxiety poured over me, which made me develop a very poor mindset, to a point where I could not recognise myself anymore.

Personally, I couldn't imagine how much more I could give and take to have a balanced and successful life at that time.

Professionally, I felt lost. I completely forgot the reason why I was working on building my businesses. However, when you have reached the bottom, the only thing you can do next is to GROW.

I let go - I stopped coaching people from my network marketing business. And delegated the majority of the work from my architecture company into the team. I needed to find out my professional and personal priorities, my vision and mission and understand what was holding me back. I needed to redefine my 'why'. I knew I had to do that before I could be ready to go back out there for anyone else again.

What should I do? Am I doing too many different things? Am I not capable of continuing my two businesses? Do I have to give up one of them, or both? All those questions consumed my mind every hour of the day.

I felt like I had been building up my own businesses during the past seven years to be able to provide for myself and my family and that now, being part of a family, I no longer needed to work for money, I had the option of staying at home to look after our baby. I felt out of place, useless.

During the first six months as a mum, I often questioned myself on whether I had a renewed sense of purpose in life. Do you ever find yourself asking that question too? I am curious:

- Why are you reading this book?
- Why is it worth your time and energy?
- How often do you check in with yourself to ask if you are still living your life with a purpose?
- What is the number one fear that is stopping you from growing right now?
- What does not feel right at this moment? And when are you going to make a decision to steer your life in a direction that feels right?

Now that this chapter is coming to an end, you might be wondering why I haven't told you what my gift is.

I still remember as a child, a girl from school telling me that the reason she did not like me was because I got on well with everyone. In her opinion, that was not possible to achieve. I have carried that painful memory with me for my entire childhood and part of my adulthood.

I never saw the harm in that, but it hurt me to be told that it wasn't natural. I do love working with people, and I absolutely love helping other women succeed.

My gift is empathy and through it, I am in the process of building my third business, CREE CONFIA CRECE - mindset and business academy for Spanish speakers and female entrepreneurs.

A business which foundation is based on the power of these three Cs:

CREE (Believe)
CONFIA (Trust)
CRECE (Grow)

Now I am ready to end this chapter, but not without giving advice to the next generation of female entrepreneurs - including my Pia. Find your gift and you will have found the purpose of your life. Never forget that growth comes with the acceptance of change.

Are you ready to accept the change and grow?

About Me

A little girl with big dreams who became a woman with vision. I love a good smile, cuddles and people. I genuinely love people.

In my own businesses, I am Founder of SPACIO architects LTD, and Brand Director at Nu Skin Enterprises. Both are consolidated online businesses operating since 2015 - one in the design and architecture industry, and the other within the network marketing business with which I help other families build a side-income that allows them to work from home and reconcile family and work life.

I am currently working on developing the female mindset and entrepreneurial movement launched in 2021, CREE CONFIA CRECE (Believe Trust Grow). This is an online business academy for Spanish speaking female entrepreneurs to improve their mindset and business systems and support them in their journey.

I dedicate this chapter to:

- You, a driven and determined reader, who has taken a first or deeper step into female entrepreneurship by getting inspired by other women's success stories. At the end of the day, we teach what we want to learn and implement ourselves.

- To my mum, my most inspirational female to follow, who with kindness and vision, has always encouraged me to dream big, and pursue my purpose in life.

- To my husband-to-be, for believing in me and being the most supportive person I have ever known, and at the same time, the person who challenges me the most.

- To Oscar, my adorable step son. Great reader and future entrepreneur, who always says to everyone with pride: "Mariana has her own businesses!"

- And last but not least, these words are especially dedicated to you, Pia, for being my dream come true. I had been creating this lifestyle a while before your arrival nine months ago, just to be ready to be me - a flexible work-from-home business mummy. The one holding your hand and enjoying seeing you grow into a kind woman with great wisdom one day.

From Disbelief To Self Belief

Luise Sargent
Counsellor
TherapyPoint.co.uk

"The future belongs to those who believe in the beauty of their dreams" -- Eleanor Roosevelt

Have you ever had that 'now or never' moment? If you don't do that thing right now you won't get another chance? Unfortunately, many of us seem to talk ourselves out of taking chances when we have these moments.

"It was never going to work anyway."

"I couldn't do that."

"What would people think?"

Well, in August 2011, I had that moment. But instead of talking myself out of it, I found myself walking into my local college in Essex to hand in an application form. I was applying to do an Access course which was the equivalent of three A Levels gained over a year of study which would allow me to fulfil my dream of going to University to train as a counsellor.

Without knowing it, that day in August was enrollment day. So before I could say or do anything, I was being whisked through the queue, asked to sign forms, and had photos taken before being sent in for an interview!

It felt so surreal. I'd had many interviews over the years - I'd worked in the city from the age of 16, however, no one had ever asked me about qualifications. So here I was sitting opposite two academics who were asking me what exams I had taken at school, 26 years previously!

I took a deep breath, swallowed, and said in a very quiet voice, "I don't have any qualifications other than an O Level in English language."

Now, regardless of the way I felt at that moment, I still think that what came out of the tutor's mouth was unacceptable. "You have no other qualifications? What, none?? How have you made it to your age without any qualifications?"

On any other day, that would have made me want to squirm and run away, but as I said, this day was different. So I replied, "Well, no one ever asked me for any!"

As I sat there wondering if I had been a bit too rude, he went on to offer me a place on the course! The only catch was, I had to take a GCSE in maths through evening classes, as well as doing the equivalent of three A Levels in just one year in order to get into university.

At this time, I was 42 with five children - three boys and twin girls. I worked part-time and as you can imagine, life was pretty hectic. So why on earth did I think taking on a degree would be a good idea? Well it was that 'now or never' moment. The girls were starting junior school and the boys were getting older. This was my time.

One of the things I remember from my day enrolling at the college was coming home with my lanyard and leaving it on the side in the kitchen. My middle son then asked me why I had a lanyard - the very same lanyard he had. I had yet to tell him that his mum was going to be at the same college as him come September! Let's just say, he wasn't ecstatic but once I explained I was assigned to a different campus to him, he was slightly less annoyed.

Two weeks later, I found myself walking into Chelmsford College, feeling like every 16 year old in the land - nervous. And then I spotted her - an older lady (well, mid 30s). I walked straight up to her and said, "You look old, are you on the Access course?"

Luckily, she didn't slap me or ignore me. Instead, she said, "Yes. I'm Bonnie, are you as terrified as me?" We instantly became friends and we supported each other through what can only be described as a highly intensive year!

One of the first essays I had to write was for my psychology class. I had this enormous textbook that I could hardly carry, let alone understand. I remember complaining about how hard the course was to a friend at the school gates and her response shocked me. "You can always give up if it's too hard."

Turns out, that was the best thing anyone could have said to me right then. It gave me the determination to succeed. Give up? I don't give up and I am not a quitter! I never have been. I remembered the words my counsellor had said to me in the past: "Luise, I'm wondering if you realise how strong you actually are?"

Not Always Strong

Ten years prior to me doing the course, I'd had some counselling, which was much needed after the breakup of my marriage. Ever since my mid-teens, I'd always put the feelings of my past boyfriends above mine.

"I don't mind what we do as long as you're happy" became my mantra and this stayed with me for years. But I wasn't being true to myself because I bloody did mind! Inside, I was angry, upset and confused but I learnt to ignore my feelings and emotions, not just to boyfriends but to friends and work colleagues too.

Now, being this type of person can be great - I was well liked, kind and considerate - but unfortunately, there are some people that will take advantage of your kind nature and manipulate things to suit them.

So this was how I found myself sitting in the doctor's surgery one day, explaining how I was feeling. He suggested I have some therapy. I knew nothing about mental health or low self-esteem so to sit in a room with a counsellor was very strange indeed. But the sessions were hugely helpful and she gave me the space to explore why I put everyone's feelings before my own. For the first time in a long time, I was heard and valued as an individual and it allowed me to take stock of my relationship, how it had made me feel and how it had shaped me as an adult.

"Luise, I'm wondering if you realise how strong you actually are?"

When my counsellor said this, I was so confused. How could I be strong? I'd allowed so much to happen to me. Despite my own beliefs, her words made me feel strong and coming out of the counsellor's office, I felt on top of the world.

I vowed to myself that this was the career for me. If I can make one person feel like she's made me feel I want to do this.

Fast forward ten years and the journey had started. Weeks slipped into months and it was very stressful. The essay writing got easier but the amount of essays got harder and harder until finally in June, it was over.

I'd earned my Diploma in Higher Education and I was all set to go to university in October 2012. But instead of celebrating, I found myself feeling defeated. My default setting was set to self-destruct.

At university, I found myself thinking again that I can't do this, it's too hard. Everyone else is better than me. I was a mature student but felt as small and scared as any child starting school! It did become easier though, mainly because of the great people I met on the course who were all going through similar journeys of self-discovery and self-doubt.

The counselling degree was very intense and it wasn't just about getting the best grade, it was about really looking at yourself, delving deep into the parts of you that have been closed off for years, the parts of you that you don't want anyone to know about. Every week we did exactly that. It was horrendous and liberating in equal measure.

I remember one of the first sessions we had where our tutor said, "You're never going to become rich being a counsellor." This didn't sit well with me.

Don't get me wrong, I hadn't gone into this as a get-rich-quick scheme and I wasn't used to having a lot of money. Growing up, we were comfortably off and had some nice holidays but money wasn't in abundance and certainly, as a parent of five children, money had become quite scarce. But there was a burning desire inside me to become financially independent and to be able to do the things I'd always wanted to do.

Putting Myself First
I quickly realised doing an intensive degree whilst working and looking after five children was bloody hard! Being organised was never my thing but I quickly worked out that

I needed to give myself a few hours a week to focus on my studies. This was where I started to understand that being in control reduced the anxiety.

Hold on, so being able to own my stuff and say I can't do [insert task] for [insert name] because I have to get this essay done, was OK? Definitely. This was the beginning of me saying I am important. I am not willing to be at the back of the queue. I have as much right to be here as you do, to be heard and to be visible.

The most shocking thing about my new found strength was that no one was disgusted by my insolence, my apparent selfishness, my ability to say no. Then the penny dropped.

This is how successful people do it. They work out what they have to do and once they've done their stuff, then, and only then, do they offer their time to others! To some it may seem ridiculous that this was a new discovery for me at 44 years old. But I bet there are quite a few of you reading this thinking, "Wow, does this mean I can be in control of my feelings and emotions too?"

Yes, it does and I am going to show you how easy it can be. But before I do that, I need to finish this darn degree.

After three years of essays and reflective writing, 100 counselling hours and an 11,000 word dissertation, it was done! It's now October 2015 and graduation day. I'm lucky enough to have my parents, partner and children with me. It was truly a special day and the best part was hearing my children say how proud they were of me.

We always tell our children how proud we are of them and how well they did but how often do your children have the opportunity to say that to you? This was a really important learning curve for me and I have spoken to many friends about this. A big part of being a mum is putting yourself last. Looking after the needs of your child and your partner becomes the norm, and over time we can forget who we are and what our needs are. So on that day it was wonderful to see how proud my children were of their mum.

I'm guessing some of you will be able to resonate with a lot of the self-doubt I've been talking about, but maybe getting back into education isn't the direction for you. This book is about growth and growth comes in many forms, but it always starts with you.

Allowing others to steer you or manipulate you, will never fulfil you. Remember the anger I felt inside? Always putting other people's needs first, feeling I didn't have a voice, feeling frustrated and resentful, I couldn't carry on living this life. I'm sure some of you have experienced similar feelings. We are born with only two fears, the fear of falling and the fear of loud noises. All the other fears you may be experiencing or have experienced have been learnt along the way. As annoying as this is, that also means that we can unlearn them.

Say that again! You can unlearn them!

A really good exercise is to look in the mirror and give yourself a compliment - difficult isn't it? Finding things we like about ourselves can be hard, really hard. But if I asked you to give me ten negatives about yourself, I'm sure they'd roll off the tongue quite easily.

Remember my counsellor, who wanted me to recognise how strong I was? I can't just decide that I feel strong, it doesn't work like that. Sometimes we have to be placed in a situation where our strength is put to the test.

I was put in that position back in September 2007. I'd remarried, my husband supported me and my three boys, and we went on to have twin daughters. Life was chaotic and stressful but I was happy.

When the girls were three, my husband had a terrible accident resulting in him being in an induced coma in a Neuro ICT unit for five weeks, and in hospital for nearly three months. All of a sudden, the strength I'd been told I had was brought to the forefront to keep everything going.

I lived in parallel worlds. The children had to be at nursery and school and I wanted to be at my husband's bedside every day. I have a fantastic family and have always felt very supported - my sisters came over from Australia and my parents from Spain, which was amazing and I will never be able to fully repay them for the sacrifices they had to make in order to support me.

But the surprising thing for me was how my friends rallied round. The hospital was a 200 mile round trip and for the first four weeks, different friends drove me there and back every single day - no questions asked. Hopefully you will never have to test your friendships in this way but this is testament to how loved I felt.

My husband luckily survived his accident and came home in November of that year. But unfortunately the brain injury made it very difficult for him to cope with everyday life - noise and chaos don't go well with a brain injury. However, these things are part and parcel of a busy house with five children, so in 2009 we decided to separate.

So here I was again, a single mum but now I had five children instead of three!

My instinct was to revert to type - I'm not complete without a man in my life, a man can make me happy, make me feel like a proper family. But this time I knew I had to do it differently. I did meet a guy who made me very happy but I made the decision that my happiness was for me to be in charge of, and what was going to make me happy was being self-sufficient in a career I loved. Hence that day in 2011, when I walked into the college.

Finding My Own Happiness

Since qualifying as a counsellor, I worked for a charity called Homestart Essex which supports families with under 5s. They offered family groups so the children could interact and learn through play but they recognised the mums needed something just for them. So I was employed to run wellbeing groups, offering a ten week course where we discussed low self-esteem, negative core beliefs, anxiety and a whole range of mental health issues that any one of us could be going through.

My role initially was tough. How do you get someone with anxiety and low self-esteem to agree to come to a group with nine other strangers and feel comfortable enough to open up? But by this time, I had started to recognise my worth and knew that what I'd been through allowed me to have empathy with these mums. Once I got them to the group I knew they'd stay. Having a creche played a major part in it and the biscuits were always great, but I was able to make them feel comfortable enough to relax and open up about how they were feeling.

I ran three groups a week for four years across mid Essex and I can honestly say I loved it. As much as I could see the difference it made for the mums, it changed my perspective in lots of ways too. It allowed me to recognise my strength. Seeing women walk in on week one with absolutely no self-worth and accepting their lot in life, resonated so much with my younger self.

To then see them on week ten become confident, independent women with opinions and voices they were not afraid to use, was absolutely thrilling. I could see myself in every single one of them. I will never forget this pivotal moment in my life which gave me the realisation that if I wanted to help women like this become independent, then I needed to be true to myself and move forward in my own life first. So with a heavy heart, I decided to move on from that role to seek the same change in myself.

I was ready for a new challenge, and although I had separated from my partner, this time, I really was looking forward to being on my own. I needed to become autonomous, to be free to make my own decisions and follow my hopes and dreams without anyone else questioning them.

So in September 2020, I took the enormous and scary decision to become fully self-employed. I really took this autonomy to the next level by starting my own business, TherapyPoint. There was no one telling me I couldn't do it, that it wouldn't work.

I sat down and wrote a business plan and worked out that I needed a certain amount of clients each week to cover my bills. I created a website, became more invested in social media and managed to triple my client base. This allowed me to invest in my business even more, which in turn, allowed me to join an entrepreneur group where I met like-minded people with their own businesses who didn't knock me but boosted me! And when I said my goal was to have a practice in Harley Street, they said, "Brilliant idea, go for it!"

So I did. I'm actually sitting in my office now at 1 Harley Street London W1 overlooking Cavendish Square while writing this chapter. This has all become a reality because I listened to my needs and ignored the self-doubt.

I would love for you to reach your goals too. My advice would be to write your own chapter, look at everything that has happened to you and use those situations, however negative they felt at the time, to recognise your own strength. I was lucky enough to have a counsellor that showed me and if that's what you need, then seek the help. But it is actually in all of us to find our own strength, we just need to believe!

My first revelation was when my counsellor made me aware of how strong I am, allowing me to look at things that had happened in my life and start to implement changes. What do you consider as your strengths? If you can't think of any right now, ask your close friends to help you see. Believe them but more importantly, believe in your own voice!

Now this chapter isn't really about me. It's about you and anyone else that has ever doubted themselves. It's for the people who allowed someone else to influence their decision or belittle their dream. You know who you are and the reason you are reading this book is because you want to do something different. You want to feel empowered and heard and valued every single day.

So maybe today is your 'now or never' day.

About Me

I am a degree qualified counsellor with a private practice in both Harley Street, London and Chelmsford in Essex. I'm a successful businesswoman and a mum to my boys who are now 30, 27 and 24, and my girls who are 17.

I believe everyone has the right to be the best possible version of themselves and if someone or something is stopping you from following your dreams then we need to reevaluate whether that person or thing should be in your life.

I would like anyone reading this book to recognise that whatever you are going through, or have been through, it doesn't have to define you. Let your dreams define you instead. Never ever give up!

Later on this year, I am moving to London to expand my business. London has always had a special place in my heart and I cannot wait to be there!

My eldest son lives in Washington DC, my middle son lives in Brighton and my youngest son and daughters live with me in Chelmsford.

My parents live in Spain and my sisters and their families are in Australia, so becoming financially independent has meant I can visit them more often than has been possible in the past.

To be part of the Queens In Business Club has given me a fantastic opportunity to open up about my hopes and dreams, and to support others but also to be supported. Being self-employed can feel incredibly isolating at times so it's really important to surround yourself with like-minded people striving for the same goals. Being chosen to write a chapter in this book has been overwhelming but I feel privileged to be part of something so amazing.

I dedicate this chapter to my children and family, because whatever has happened, you have always been there for me and given me the strength to keep going.

Conclusion

After reading this series of powerful growth stories, we hope that you can see that no matter what life throws your way, there is always a choice or opportunity. We can choose to let hurdles hinder us, or we can choose to learn from them.

We hope that you can apply this thinking to your own experiences to help you go from strength to strength, no matter what challenges come your way.

- What are some of the obstacles or fears that you currently face, or have faced in the past?
- How did you react to these moments and can you identify any limiting beliefs that you have internalised?
- How can you view what happened in a different light?
- What hidden lessons are there to reflect on?
- How can you use your experiences to help others who are going through something similar?
- How can your experience help you grow as a person?

Life is always going to be full of ups and downs. It is important to acknowledge that sometimes we need to rest and reflect in order to heal from difficulty. But we must not dwell in this space.

There is something to be learned or gained from our experiences, whether they inspire us to learn new skills to avoid future mistakes, or whether they help shift our mindset to be better able to cope with future challenges. If we can approach life this way, we can continue fulfilling our purpose and become ultimately unstoppable.

About Queens In Business

Our Why

Today women are making waves in the world of entrepreneurship. There have never been more women rising up, standing up for what they believe in and building their own vehicle for freedom.

It's our belief that each and every woman has what it takes to be successful. Everyone has a gift inside of them, a skill or knowledge that could help someone who is struggling right now.

Women have the ability to contribute to the world and deserve the opportunity to be successful, feel fulfilled and have the freedom to start or scale their own business.

As women, we have always been nurturers and problem solvers – it's in our biology and many of us spend our lives thinking of others and putting others first. But who is looking after us?

The journey of entrepreneurship can be challenging at times and with just a fraction of women taking the leap to start their own businesses it can be a lonely ride.

That's why we created the Queens In Business Club.

The Queens In Business Club is more than just a community. It's a movement created to recognise the achievements of women, to support and guide female entrepreneurs and give them the tools to build and grow their own successful businesses.

Co-founded by five of us, it's the first of its kind, created by female entrepreneurs for female entrepreneurs:

Chloë Bisson – The Automation Queen
Carrie Griffiths – The Speaking Queen
Shim Ravalia – The Health Queen
Sunna Coleman – The Writing Queen
Tanya Grant – The Branding Queen

Before starting the QIB Club, we'd all built our own successful businesses, spent huge amounts of money on training and mentorship and invested years in growing our businesses.

We learned and mastered specific strategies and methods to get our businesses where they are today and we are now sharing those learnings and experiences with the members of the QIB Club.

Whether it is having a successful business or becoming financially independent, we aim to provide female entrepreneurs with the tools they need and a community to support them along the way.

Our Methodology
We believe that in business the ability to achieve success comes down to three core pillars:

244

- Education
- Empowerment
- Execution

Education for us means having the right skills, knowledge and strategies to achieve your goals and if you don't have them right now, having access to learn from experts that do.

Empowerment is about surrounding yourself with the right people to support you and cheer for you on the journey. It is about creating an empowering environment that nourishes you to be the best that you can be.

Execution means having the motivation, determination and drive to do what it takes to get to your end goal. Where we may struggle to find the motivation within ourselves, it's about having mentors to encourage you and giving you a kick up the bum when you need it.

At Queens In Business, we've created a powerful methodology that combines all three of the core pillars.

We provide the hands-on business education from world class experts with the push you need to execute your strategies whilst surrounding you with supportive members to empower you to overcome any roadblocks that come up on the way.

Our Mission
We're on a mission to change the world of entrepreneurship.

We want to create a movement that empowers women and encourages their drive for success, not belittles it or judges them for putting their career first.

We want to eliminate the fear of judgement and the fear of failure. We want to create a world where it's OK to ask for help, it's OK to express your challenges and it's OK to make mistakes.

We want to support women in becoming powerful role models for their children, paving the path of the future generations of women who will believe in their abilities and believe they can achieve what they want.

It's our mission to provide support to Queens all over the world regardless of their age, background, or their position in their business. Whether they want to take their business to the next level or just get started, there is always a place for them in our community.

It's time now for women to rise up and be leaders, fight for what they want for themselves and for others.

We are determined to rise.

To find out more about the Queens In Business Club, go to:
www.queensinbusinessclub.com
Contact us on:
team@queensinbusinessclub.com